BREWING WITH
CANNABIS

USING THC AND
CBD IN BEER

T0168217

BY KEITH VILLA, Ph.D.

BREWERS
PUBLICATIONS.

Brewers Publications®
A Division of the Brewers Association
PO Box 1679, Boulder, Colorado 80306-1679
BrewersAssociation.org
BrewersPublications.com

Proudly Printed in the United States of America.
10 9 8 7 6 5 4 3 2 1
ISBN-13: 978-1-938469-69-5
ISBN-10: 1-93-846969-0
EISBN: 978-1-938469-70-1

Library of Congress Control Number: 2021938107

Publisher: Kristi Switzer
Copyediting: Iain Cox
Indexing: Doug Easton
Art Direction, Interior Design: Jason Smith
Production: Justin Petersen
Cover Photo: Luke Trautwein
Illustrations: Cory Campbell

To Finn B. Knudsen and Professor Charles A. Masschelein, who convinced me to change career paths from "people doctor" to "beer doctor".

TABLE OF CONTENTS

NOTE FROM
THE PUBLISHER

This is the first of two books exploring the intersection of cannabis and beer. Cannabis is the name of the plant grown primarily for two products: the stem fiber product hemp, and the intoxicating resinous product marijuana. Consequently, depending on the reason it is being cultivated, the terms "hemp" and "marijuana" are often used to denote the cannabis plant itself. However, it is important to maintain a distinction between the two. Marijuana is cannabis that contains more than 0.3% tetrahydrocannabinol (THC) by dry weight. Hemp is cannabis that contains not more than 0.3% THC by dry weight. THC is the compound responsible for the inebriating effect of marijuana. Marijuana remains illegal under federal law, though currently 42 US states, Puerto Rico, Guam, and the District of Columbia have made at least some allowances for medical and/or recreational use under their laws. Hemp, on the other hand, is legal under federal law and its use in brewing will be the subject of an upcoming book.

Despite "cannabis" encompassing both hemp and marijuana, the subject of this book is marijuana—the higher THC-containing plant and its products. It is important to note that over half of all drug arrests in the United States between 2001 and 2010 have been attributed to possession of marijuana. The majority of these arrests have disproportionately targeted the Black community, despite usage rates for marijuana among Black Americans being on a par with white Americans. [1] It's also important to acknowledge that there is also a history of vilifying the plant by playing upon anti-immigrant sentiment. This context led us to carefully consider the language we would use in working on this subject. Considering the history of word choice, we also needed to balance using language that offers the clearest understanding of *Cannabis* in all its iterations.

Going forward in this book, we will be using the term *Cannabis* (capitalized, italics) when referring to the genus or species of that genus; and cannabis when referring to the plant in general or the plant's cultivation in general. We will use the term marijuana when referring to the processed plant product that has psychoactive properties, especially in the legal context. You may see the term "Marihuana" noted in specific laws or quotations and this reflects the spelling used in legislation. Lastly, we will use (industrialized) hemp when referring to the cultivated cannabis plant that has not more than 0.3% THC by dry weight.

The Brewers Association does not encourage illegal activity by anyone, including members of the brewing community. The reader accordingly should note that the possession and use of marijuana or its components (e.g., THC extract) remains a serious federal crime as of the date of this book's publication. Even in the context of certain hemp byproducts (most notably cannabidiol, or CBD), use commercially in food and drinks remain subject to adverse federal action at this time, as the federal Food & Drug Administration has not yet recognized CBD and similar byproducts as either dietary supplements or ingredients "generally recognized as safe." Nevertheless, many observers believe that the federal government will legalize marijuana and recognize food and/or supplement uses for byproducts like CBD within the next few years. Moreover, interest in the potential for beverages infused with cannabis plant derivatives runs high in the alcohol beverage industry, and has attracted substantial investment from established players within the industry. As such, the Brewers Association perceives a very real impending need to educate the brewing community at large about this emerging and rapidly-changing subject.

Finally, it is important to advise the reader that combining two intoxicants like alcohol and THC involves risks in addition to those normally associated with each substance separately. And at least partly because of the illegal status of marijuana, science and medicine may not completely understand those

---

[1] "The War on Marijuana in Black and White," American Civil Liberties Union, June 2013, https://www.aclu.org/files/assets/061413-mj-report-rfs-rel4.pdf.

added risks. As such, in the interest of safety, we offer considerable information in this book on how to make non-alcoholic beer. The book does offer recipes for beer combined with THC, but even after legalization (if that ever occurs) **the reader should only attempt these recipes at their own discretion after carefully considering the most up-to-date information on the risks of combining alcohol with THC.**

This book will serve as a snapshot in time and every effort has been made to ensure it is up to date at the time it goes to press. But, as already highlighted, both the applicable laws and our knowledge of the various benefits and risks of cannabis use are changing rapidly. Readers should be sure to do their research before embarking on this journey.

Kristi Switzer
Publisher, Brewers Publications
May 17, 2021

ACKNOWLEDGMENTS

This book would not have been possible without the support of my wife Jodi, and kids Catherine, Marie, and Kevin. Additionally, a huge amount of gratitude to all my friends, relatives, fellow brewers, and cannabis aficionados around the world who provided the inspiration. Ed Rosenthal and Mason Hembree—thank you for your pioneering work so that others, like me, could follow. Finally, Kristi Switzer, my weekly cheerleader, advisor, and journalistic sage, otherwise known as "the Publisher," provided much needed coaching to get this over the goal line!

INTRODUCTION

When I was first asked to write this book, I was hesitant. Not because writing a book is difficult, although it is. Rather, the concept of trying to gather practical information on a plant that is illegal under US federal law and trying to take a snapshot of a subject area that evolves weekly, even daily, might well be described as a fool's errand. However, after much consideration it became clear that a thorough and thoughtful collation of current knowledge about the technical and legal aspects of brewing with cannabis—from a brewer's perspective—could help align the craft beer industry on some incredibly important considerations and decisions that may ultimately impact the entire brewing industry. That's the upside.

The downside is the possibility of this book being seen as encouraging brewers to combine ethanol and THC into single products.[1] A brief reflection on the fate of products involving ethanol and caffeine (a much less controversial and much less potent bioactive molecule) should make clear to everyone in the industry that **a decision to pre-combine ethanol and THC is highly unwise** at this time. That said, homebrewers have been experimenting with marijuana in beer for ages and the fact is that those experiments are ongoing. Brewers Publications and I offer this work in the hopes of helping to shape the future of this topic, rather than to react to and be shaped by the risk takers among us.

---

[1] THC stands for tetrahydrocannabinol, specifically delta-9-tetrahydrocannabinol, which is the most common psychoactive phytocannabinoid in the marijuana plant.

With this in mind, this book is an attempt to provide practical information to craft brewers so that we can apply our extensive collective knowledge about hops to its botanical cousin.

The first chapter provides an introduction to the world of marijuana. It also provides some historical context, showing how marijuana became illegal under federal law in the 1930s, which criminalized its use and possession, and the subsequent moves by individual US states in more recent decades to decriminalize and even fully legalize marijuana use. The glossary (p. 167) can be used as a companion to become acquainted with important terms and technical jargon used throughout this book, including, for example, THC used above, the primary psychoactive chemical in marijuana.

Chapter 2 covers the basics of cannabis biology. Additionally, the similarities between plants of the *Cannabis* and *Humulus* genera (cannabis and hops, respectively) are reviewed. Chapter 3 deals with the agronomy of marijuana, discussing the cannabis plant's unique characteristics and presenting some theories as to why it produces compounds such as cannabinoids and terpenes. The active components of marijuana and their chemistry with regard to agronomics are also covered.

Chapters 4 and 5 discuss how cannabinoids and terpenes in marijuana function and how to use them in beverages. Chapter 6 is the legal chapter that presents a top-level view of the current legal status of marijuana in the US. Chapter 7 covers packaging, labeling, and sales and marketing and what is and is not allowed in those states where recreational marijuana is legal.

It is illegal to offer for sale alcohol and marijuana together in the same beverage in the US. While non-alcoholic beers present fewer legal obstacles, fashioning a non-alcoholic beer that is appealing to beer drinkers is no easy feat. Additionally, it cannot be stressed enough how critical it is to pasteurize or stabilize these types of beers so that consumers are not exposed to products that may sicken them. Chapter 8 gives an overview of the procedures currently in use by breweries around the world to create non-alcoholic beers. It covers something as simple as stove-top boiling off of ethanol, which a homebrewer can easily achieve, to the high-tech methods, such as reverse osmosis or vacuum distillation, that larger breweries routinely use.

Chapter 9 presents brewing recipes, both extract-based and all-grain, that brewers can adapt or use as guidance when creating beers with marijuana in states where it is legal. This chapter also describes how to decarboxylate tetrahydrocannabinolic acid (THCA, the precursor to THC) into the fully psychoactive form of THC.

Chapter 10, the final chapter, is meant to give the reader inspiration for the future. The discovery of new cannabinoids and terpenes may lead to a better understanding of how marijuana can be used.

I hope this book will ultimately be useful to readers interested in learning more about marijuana and the cannabis plant. This collation of existing knowledge is meant to provide a common baseline for brewers if, or when, it becomes appropriate to market non-alcoholic beverages with marijuana.

1

MARIJUANA LAWS IN THE UNITED STATES: A BRIEF HISTORY

THE CRUSADE AGAINST MARIJUANA

Upon gazing at a fully mature cannabis plant and imagining the hundreds of years it has been used for fabric, rope, paper, and social relaxation, among many other things, few people can imagine the powerful political and monetary motives that were put in place to isolate marijuana as an illegal drug in the US. For the story of how marijuana became associated with undesirable people, illegal activities, and immoral behaviors and was eventually classified as a Schedule I substance under the Controlled Substances Act, we begin with the secretary of the US Department of the Treasury during the early 1930s.

The secretary of the Treasury at that time was a man named Andrew Mellon. Mellon's family also owned one of the largest US banks of the early twentieth century, Mellon Bank, headquartered in Pittsburgh, Pennsylvania. In turn, Mellon Bank was the majority owner of Gulf Oil Corporation, also headquartered in Pittsburgh, which was a relatively new business supplying gasoline to the emerging automobile market. Mellon Bank was concurrently a large investor in the DuPont chemical company, which supplied chemicals to the tree-based paper industry, critical to newspaper production.

At that time, a man by the name of William Randolph Hearst was heavily invested in newspapers in the US. Hearst was one of the most powerful men in America whose newspaper empire provided news to 17% of the American public. In other words, in the 1930s approximately 20 million Americans obtained their view of the world's news from one of Hearst's newspapers (Nasaw 2000, xiv). Of course, this was prior to the advent of television and radio, when newspapers dominated the news market.

With this background in mind, the seemingly innocent cannabis plant, specifically hemp, was uniquely placed as a single source of products that could threaten the profits and existence of Gulf Oil Corporation, DuPont, and Hearst Enterprises. Gulf Oil was positioning itself to sell gasoline from its oil fields in Texas to motorists in drive-up gas stations, a relatively new concept to offer convenience to automobile drivers. At around the same time, engineers from the Ford Motor Company had discovered that biofuel could be made from the hemp plant in a sustainable manner to provide a non-fossil fuel solution to power their automobiles. This valuable discovery meant that Ford could derive profit from both the sale of their cars and a novel fuel source to power them.

Figure 1.1. Ford designer Lowell E. Overly in the Soybean Car, made from soybean, hemp, and other plants, August 1941. *From the Collections of the Henry Ford (ID 64.167.189.P.16353).*

As an aside, Ford also believed that bioplastics could be made from hemp and other agricultural crops. The company studied these bioplastics and found them to be very strong, even constructing a car body entirely from bioplastic made from soybean, hemp, and other plants.[1] The car was called the 1941 Soybean Car (fig 1.1). Unfortunately, Ford's research in this area was halted during World War II and was never reactivated.

Hearst's newspaper empire was heavily invested in the timber industry and thereby highly dependent on DuPont's chemical process for turning wood fiber into suitable paper for newsprint. This was in spite of the fact that DuPont's process produced paper that was inferior and turned yellow over time, compared to the high-quality white paper that could be obtained from hemp fiber. Hemp-based paper was also more sustainable than wood-based paper. Even today, paper made from wood using modern technology can only be recycled three times before it is unusable, while hemp-based paper can be recycled seven to eight times (Małachowska et al. 2015, 135). To protect their interests, DuPont and Hearst teamed up and began a campaign to sully and disparage the image of the cannabis/hemp plant. DuPont heavily lobbied the US Congress to take on a negative view of cannabis, while casting a positive view on the timber-based paper industry.

Hearst-owned newspapers began a not-so-subtle smear campaign to convince the American public and congressional officials of the dangers of marijuana. They began by using the word "marihuana" as a direct substitute for the word "hemp," which was the common name at the time for the cannabis plant. Through association, this new term became synonymous with a dangerous, addictive drug. The smear campaign was also successful in associating marijuana use with racial minorities during the period when the eugenics movement, white supremacy, and the Ku Klux Klan were gaining momentum.

The Federal Bureau of Narcotics (FBN), established in 1930 as an agency of the Treasury, took notice. Coincidentally, the commissioner of the FBN was Harry J. Anslinger, the husband of Andrew Mellon's niece and personally appointed to be commissioner by Mellon himself. Anslinger would serve as FBN head for more than 30 years. In 1937 Anslinger stated, "Marijuana is the most violence causing drug in the history of mankind. Most marijuana smokers are Negroes, Hispanics, Filipinos and entertainers. Their Satanic music, jazz and swing, result from marijuana usage. This marijuana causes white women to seek sexual relations with Negroes" (quoted in Gerber 2004, 9). He also wrote an article for the

---

[1]   "Pinch Hitters for Defense," *Popular Mechanics*, December 1941, 3.

Marihuana versus Marijuana

The different spellings of *marihuana/marijuana* date back to the 1930s and are attributed to those seeking prohibition of cannabis (Lee 2012, 51). Prior to this, the plant was known as hemp or cannabis.* Mexicans colloquially referred to the plant as *marijuana* and most likely spelled it with a *j*. However, in order to win proponents onto the side of prohibition, the Spanish terms marijuana and marihuana were used in order to associate the plant with Mexicans and take advantage of the prejudice that existed after the Spanish-American War (Hudak 2020, 24). In spoken Spanish, the letter *j* has the same pronunciation as the letter *h*, and so both spellings were used interchangeably. When the Federal Bureau of Narcotics—precursor to the Drug Enforcement Administration (DEA)—prohibited cannabis in 1937 it chose to use the *h* spelling, conceivably to force the Spanish pronunciation and enforce the negative connotations (Hudak 2020, 25). Ever since then, the DEA has used both spellings interchangeably when updating or providing further guidance. Notably, with the legalization of marijuana in Michigan under the Michigan Regulation and Taxation of Marihuana Act of 2018, the archaic spelling *marihuana* was chosen to be used in the wording of the law. Other states have adopted the *j* spelling for legalization efforts.

* Christopher Ingraham, "'Marijuana' or 'marihuana'? It's all weed to the DEA," *Washington Post*, December 16, 2016, 6:00 a.m. CST, https://www.washingtonpost.com/news/wonk/wp/2016/12/16 /marijuana-or-marihuana-its-all-weed-to-the-dea/.

Benevolent Protective Order of the Elks in which he described marijuana as "one of the most dangerous and depraving narcotics known" and that "the consumption of one marijuana cigarette is sufficient to push the psycho-neurotic type of person from sanity to madness" (DEA 2018, 19). Most of Anslinger's accusations and assertions, although non-scientific, lurid, and rooted in racial prejudice, were taken seriously and swayed congressional and public opinion against the use of marijuana while not realizing that hemp, cannabis, and marijuana were one and the same.

Anslinger took further steps by authoring a new bill and getting it introduced into the House of Representatives, and then having this marijuana tax bill slipped through the House Ways and Means Committee and Senate Finance Committee for consideration before being signed into law by President Roosevelt. In other words, this "backdoor" method allowed Anslinger to create a law with minimal consultation and minimal debate by either political party. Many were unaware that hemp was included in the bill because of the use of the term "marihuana," which people did not realize was a different name for the same plant at that time. The American Medical Association argued that marijuana was not an addictive drug and that the new legislation unfairly penalized doctors who prescribed it, pharmacists who prepared it, and farmers who grew it. Nevertheless, the bill was passed into law as the Marihuana Tax Act of 1937, which placed a tax on the sale of cannabis and led to the prohibition of marijuana and hemp.

The Marihuana Tax Act required that a yearly tax of $24 be paid by cannabis suppliers and importers and that all supplies of cannabis were to be registered and marked with a tax stamp (fig. 1.2). Any attempts to circumvent the law were met with a fine of up to $2,000 and/or up to five years in prison. On October 3, 1937 in Denver, Colorado, two people were arrested for the first time under the new law for not paying marijuana tax: Moses Baca and Samuel Caldwell. Baca received a sentence of 18 months for possession, while Caldwell received a four-year sentence. Both men were imprisoned in the US penitentiary at Leavenworth, Kansas, and their names and images are today sometimes found on t-shirts and other paraphernalia for being the first people to suffer under the new law.[2] By treating cannabis as an illegal, highly addictive drug, and by implementing the Marihuana Tax Act, the FBN effectively eliminated the recreational use of marijuana in the United States. This law was in force until 1969, when it was ruled unconstitutional.

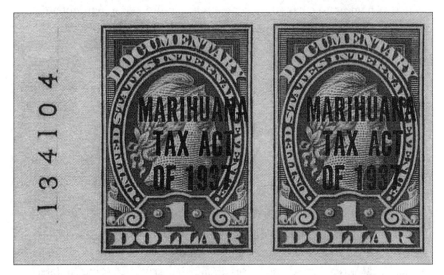

Figure 1.2. 1937 Marihuana Tax Stamps issued by the US federal government to identify that taxes were paid for cannabis. *U.S. Bureau of Engraving and Printing; Imaging by Gwillhickers, Public domain, via Wikimedia Commons.*

---

[2]   Daniel Glick, "Marijuana Prohibition Began With These Arrests in 1937," *Leafly*, October 2, 2017, https://www.leafly.com/news/politics/drug-war-prisoners-1-2-true-story-moses-sam-two-denver-drifters-became-cannabis-pioneers.

In 1969, in the case of *Leary v. United States*, the Supreme Court found that the 1937 act was a violation of the Fifth Amendment because obtaining a legal tax stamp involved admitting guilt in violating the law, that is, self-incrimination. As a result, Congress acted quickly to find a legal way to keep marijuana and other drugs off the streets and out of the hands of anyone wanting to enjoy or experiment with them. Within months, Congress passed the Controlled Substances Act of 1970, which classified drugs into five different schedules based on their medical value and their potential for addiction and abuse.[3] Experts from the healthcare and drug manufacturing industries were consulted for their opinions regarding placement of drugs into the original schedule classifications, I–V. Needless to say, due to the illegal nature of marijuana, it had not been thoroughly studied with regard to its addictiveness or medical value. Rather, all of the historical arguments against the cannabis plant were used in arguments to classify marijuana as a dangerous and addictive Schedule I drug.

The term "abuse" is ill-defined, and yet "the abuse rate is a determinate factor in the scheduling of the drug."[4] Schedule V drugs are defined as having the least potential for abuse and include items such as cough syrups with less than 200 mg codeine per 100 mL. Schedule I drugs are the most dangerous and defined as having no currently accepted medical use and a high potential for abuse. Some examples of Schedule I drugs include heroin, LSD, ecstasy, and cannabis. The United States Drug Enforcement Agency (DEA) was founded in 1973 to enforce the Controlled Substances Act. Since then, many people have been prosecuted for the use and possession of cannabis. It is estimated that, currently, more than half of all drug arrests in the US are due to marijuana. Furthermore, racial minorities and marijuana consumption are still linked together in a very negative manner and there remains a strong element of racial bias—data from 2001 to 2010 show that Black people are 3.73 times more likely than white people to be arrested for marijuana charges.[5]

MAKING MARIJUANA LEGAL

In spite of the decades-long federal prohibition of marijuana, the majority of states in the US have since passed laws that legalize the use of marijuana for medical and/or recreational purposes. In fact, by early 2021 some 36 states and

---

3   "Drug Scheduling," Drug Enforcement Administration, accessed November 30, 2020,
     https://www.dea.gov/drug-scheduling.
4   "Drug Scheduling," Drug Enforcement Administration.
5   "Marijuana Arrests by the Numbers," ACLU, accessed November 30, 2020,
     https://www.aclu.org/gallery/marijuana-arrests-numbers.

four US territories had legalized medical marijuana, with 16 of those states and the District of Columbia having also made recreational marijuana legal. In the discussion that follows (and throughout this book), the terms "fully state legal" and "fully state legalized" denote the legalization of both medical marijuana and recreational marijuana. The term "decriminalization" means that a person caught possessing small amounts of marijuana will receive a ticket and a fine, rather than arrest and jail time.

Decriminalization of Marijuana in the US

Oregon was the first to experiment with legalization when they decriminalized marijuana with the Oregon Decriminalization Bill of 1973. This bill made the possession of up to one ounce of marijuana a violation rather than a crime, which was punishable by a civil fine of up to $100 (Blachly 1976). There were stipulations that came with the law, such as possession within 1,000 feet of a school or driving under the influence, that remained unchanged and were classified as criminal acts. After decriminalization, the issue of marijuana legalization was debated in the Oregon court system for many years. Finally, an emergency bill was signed into law by the governor that legalized the sale of recreational marijuana, starting October 1, 2015. From that point onward, both recreational and medical marijuana have been fully legal in Oregon.

The state of Alaska also has a history of early decriminalization of marijuana. In 1975, a man named Irwin Ravin was arrested for possession of marijuana. In *Ravin v. State*, Ravin argued that the use of marijuana was protected by his state and federal right to privacy, especially since there was no scientific evidence that marijuana was a dangerous drug. After a thorough investigation of the literature, the Supreme Court of Alaska found that there was no evidence marijuana posed a danger to the user or to others, and that the sanctity and privacy of activities within one's home far outweighed the perceived dangers of marijuana (Brandeis 2012, 179–180). The court weighed the (almost sacred) right to privacy in Alaska against the lack of any literature-based evidence of danger from marijuana and decided to decriminalize it.

The Alaskan court's decision allowed for a civil fine of no more than $100 for the possession of less than one ounce of marijuana in public and the possession of any amount for private use within a person's home, but the decision did not legalize marijuana use while driving or for minors and it also prohibited the sale of marijuana. In 1982, the court clarified the ruling by stating that a maximum amount of four ounces was allowed and that civil fines would be eliminated. This ruling allowed for the possession of a fairly large amount of marijuana, and the freedom to enjoy it at any time, which was as close to legalization as a state could get in 1982. Unfortunately, decriminalization in Alaska was short-lived, as 1990 brought about the complete illegalization of marijuana. The 1990 Alaska Marijuana Criminalization Initiative, also called Measure 2, was passed by voters and had heavy federal backing. It made all marijuana possession illegal, with penalties of up to 90 days in jail and/or up to a $1,000 fine.[6]

The 1980s and 1990s was a time when the so-called war on drugs was being waged in a bid to eliminate recreational drug use in the US. Bills were being introduced to the US Congress such as H.R. 5293, also called the Anti-Drug Abuse Act of 1990, which was designed to "eliminate the scourge of illegal drugs and fight drug abuse."[7] After the passage of Alaska's Measure 2 in 1990, marijuana decriminalization and legalization efforts renewed and wound their way through the state's court system for many years. Ironically, in 2014 the same name "Measure 2" was used for a bill that would "tax and regulate the production, sale, and use of marijuana in Alaska." Fortunately for the many cannabis aficionados in Alaska, this Measure 2 passed and the recreational use and possession of marijuana became fully legalized. In Alaska, the first legal sale of marijuana in dispensaries took place on October 29, 2016.[8]

Individual State Legalization

Looking past decriminalization and toward legalization, the legalization of cannabis/marijuana in individual states can be traced back to 1996 when California passed the Compassionate Use Act (Proposition 215), which legalized medical cannabis. This law allowed for anyone with an ailment for which marijuana provided relief to use, possess and grow cannabis, although it required a physician's approval. Legalization in California inspired cannabis users around the country to try to pass similar legislation to approve the use of medical marijuana in their own states. Over time, it became clear that full legalization of marijuana was the ultimate goal of many users and organizers.

---

[6]   "Alaska Voters Approve Measure to Recriminalize Marijuana," the Associated Press, November 7, 1990, https://apnews.com/article/4db1bf97a3d7c3a94c1d1e304f149c06.

[7]   Anti-Drug Abuse Act of 1990, H.R. 5293, 101st Cong. (1989-1990), https://www.congress.gov/bill /101st-congress/house-bill/5293/titles.

[8]   "Alaska Marijuana Legalization, Ballot Measure 2 (2014)," Ballotpedia, accessed November 30, 2020, https://ballotpedia.org/Alaska_Marijuana_Legalization,_Ballot_Measure_2_(2014); "Alaska becomes 3rd state with legal marijuana," USA Today, February 24, 2015, 12:59 a.m. ET, https://www.usatoday.com/story/news/nation/2015/02/24/alaska-legal-marijuana/23922313 /; Associated Press, "Alaska Shop Set to Offer State's First Legal Marijuana Sales," Fortune, October 29, 2016, 10:45 a.m. CDT, https://fortune.com/2016/10/29/alaska-legal-marijuana-sales/.

With this in mind, when the shift to legalization happened, it happened quickly. The state of Washington was the first to legalize recreational marijuana, doing so on December 6, 2012 with the passage of Initiative 502; four days later, Colorado's Amendment 64 went into effect, which legalized the recreational cannabis market in the state. Many other states have followed suit in one way or another. In fact, by early 2021, 36 states and four US territories had legalized medical marijuana, of which 16 states and the District of Columbia had also made recreational marijuana legal (*see* table 1.1 in next section). Since 2012, practically every election cycle has shown that states are willing to put the question of cannabis legalization on the ballot. In addition to cannabis industry leaders who believe federal legalization will occur in the near future, Senator Chuck Schumer (D-NY), Senator Cory Booker (D-NJ), and Senator Ron Wyden (D-OR) released a statement on February 1, 2021 stating their intention to introduce "comprehensive cannabis reform legislation."[9]

However, while some believe federal legalization will occur as early as 2022 or 2024, there are others who believe it will not happen for a long time because, among the many possible reasons, the current situation with Internal Revenue Code Sec. 280E results in a financial windfall for the federal government.[10] Federal legalization could erode this lucrative source of funds. Sec. 280E means that a taxpayer trafficking in Schedule I or Schedule II drugs can only deduct the cost of goods sold from taxable income. Costs for other business expenses—such as advertising, marketing, etc.—cannot be deducted (McElroy 2014). Remarkably, the Internal Revenue Code does not differentiate between income derived from legal sources and income derived from illegal sources. Therefore, because of Sec. 280E, it is estimated that the effective tax rate for cannabis businesses is estimated to be about 70% and that the legal cannabis market in the US generates about $1.3 billion in tax revenue per year. Given the size of the illegal and legal cannabis markets combined is estimated to be worth about $40 billion, an estimated $28 billion in taxes could be expected to be generated in the US.[11]

---

9   David Grosso and Oliver Spurgeon, "Shift in Political Power in Washington DC Sets Up Profound Changes to Federal Cannabis Laws," Arent Fox, February 16, 2021, https://www.arentfox.com/perspectives/alerts/shift-political-power-washington-dc-sets-profound-changes-federal-cannabis-laws.

10   Expenditures in connection with the illegal sale of drugs, 26 U.S.C. § 280E (2018), https://www.govinfo.gov/content/pkg/USCODE-2018-title26/html/USCODE-2018-title26-subtitleA-chap1-subchapB-partIX-sec280E.htm.

11   Pat Oglesby, "280E Revenue Cost," Future Cannabis Project, November 22, 2016, http://futurecannabisproject.org/2016/11/280e-revenue-cost/.

Agriculture Improvement Act

Almost 50 years after the passage of the Controlled Substances Act, the US government passed the Agriculture Improvement Act of 2018 (also called the 2018 farm bill), thereby identifying two subcategories of cannabis: hemp and marijuana. The Agriculture Improvement Act made legal throughout the United States the possession and selling of certain hemp-derived products, such as oil or parts of the plant that do not contain cannabinoids (discussed further in chapter 5). However, the act specified that hemp plants are legal only when they contain less than 0.3% THC as total dry weight.[12] The new distinction between marijuana and hemp was not based on science or recommendations from experts. Rather, it was based on a previous, best-guess dividing line that was used to study the biology of hemp and marijuana (Small and Cronquist 1976). Not surprisingly, researcher Ernest Small, who first proposed using the 0.3% distinction, did not intend for this to be a legal limit and was quoted as saying, "At that time, when I did that study and published it, I had no idea that that would be used as a practical measure for countries licensing the amount of THC that would be permitted in order to grow it" (Israel 2018). This has resulted in expensive forfeitures of hemp crops, including over 40% of Arizona hemp farmers in 2019 being forced to destroy entire hemp harvests that exceeded 0.3% THC.[13]

Under the Agriculture Improvement Act, cannabis plants containing more than 0.3% THC as total dry weight are classified as marijuana/marihuana and remain illegal under federal law in the US market.

CURRENT STATUS OF MARIJUANA IN THE LAW

Marijuana remains illegal under federal law. It is legal under state law in a majority of states (see discussion above and also in chapter 6). These limited, state-specific legal markets are often comprised of two distinct subcategories—medical and recreational marijuana—both of which are regulated through state-licensed dispensaries. The medical marijuana market, as of April 2021 approved in 36 US states and the District of Columbia, is aimed at those who require it for pain relief or relief from debilitating illnesses, such as cancer and epilepsy. Additionally, many people can obtain medical permits for consuming marijuana, as long as a doctor approves it, whether justified by a thorough examination or at the simple request of the patient.

---

[12] total THC as dry weight = delta-9-THC + (THCA × 0.877)

[13] "Tests Find Some Early Arizona Hemp Crops Have Too Much THC," Associated Press, January 19, 2020, https://apnews.com/article/11bed04631137ca111d64cf518d3d2bf.

Although intended only for adults over the age of 21, some states allow for people as young as 18 to obtain medical permits for marijuana without parental permission. Predictably, some adults under the age of 21 have been known to relocate to states with legal marijuana markets for "medical" reasons or to obtain post-secondary education in a state where they can procure a medical marijuana permit. More sobering are the numerous accounts of patients with cancer or debilitating diseases who move because they truly need access to marijuana for medical reasons, or those parents who risk everything to take their epileptic children for treatment to states that allow medical marijuana.

As of April 2021, the recreational marijuana market had been approved in 16 states and the District of Columbia. These markets allow for the possession and consumption of marijuana by anyone over the age of 21. Many of these "Rec" states also allow for the growing of cannabis plants for personal consumption (discussed more in chapter 6). Table 1.1 shows the states and federal district where either medical or recreational or both types of marijuana consumption are legal (the complete table can be seen in chapter 6).

Table 1.1 The legal status of marijuana by state, showing whether it is legalized for medical or recreational use

State	Legal Status	Medical	Decriminalized
Alaska	Fully Legal	Yes	Yes
Arizona	Fully Legal	Yes	Yes
Arkansas	Mixed	Yes	No
California	Fully Legal	Yes	Yes
Colorado	Fully Legal	Yes	Yes
Connecticut	Mixed	Yes	Yes
Delaware	Mixed	Yes	Yes
District of Columbia	Fully Legal	Yes	Yes
Florida	Mixed	Yes	No
Hawaii	Mixed	Yes	Yes
Illinois	Fully Legal	Yes	Yes
Louisiana	Mixed	Yes	No
Maine	Fully Legal	Yes	Yes
Maryland	Mixed	Yes	Yes
Massachusetts	Fully Legal	Yes	Yes

State	Legal Status	Medical	Decriminalized
Michigan	Fully Legal	Yes	Yes
Minnesota	Mixed	Yes	Yes
Mississippi	Mixed	Yes	Yes
Missouri	Mixed	Yes	Yes
Montana	Fully Legal[a]	Yes	Yes[a]
Nevada	Fully Legal	Yes	Yes
New Hampshire	Mixed	Yes	Yes
New Jersey	Fully Legal	Yes	Yes
New Mexico	Mixed	Yes	Yes
New York	Fully Legal	Yes	Yes
North Dakota	Mixed	Yes	Yes
Ohio	Mixed	Yes	Yes
Oklahoma	Mixed	Yes	No
Oregon	Fully Legal	Yes	Yes
Pennsylvania	Mixed	Yes	No
Rhode Island	Mixed	Yes	Yes
South Dakota	Fully Legal[a]	Yes[a]	Yes[a]
Utah	Mixed	Yes	No
Vermont	Fully Legal	Yes	Yes
Virginia	Mixed	CBD Oil Only	Yes
Washington	Fully Legal	Yes	Yes
West Virginia	Mixed	Yes	No

Source: "Map of Marijuana Legality by State," DISA, accessed May 3, 2021, https://disa.com/map-of-marijuana-legality-by-state.

Notes: State status reflects current laws as of April 2021. "Fully legal" status means marijuana is allowed for both medicinal and recreational use.

[a] Enactment is pending until future date.

Although it has been nine years since full legalization in Colorado and Washington state, the negative outcomes predicted by marijuana prohibitionists have not been seen. In fact, underage use of marijuana has been reported to decrease after legalization (Anderson et al. 2019). Additionally, states with legal markets have seen increased revenue from taxing marijuana, with sales tax rates as high as 37% (Boesen 2020, 7). As an example, the state of Colorado has seen tax revenue in excess of $1 billion since legalization; as required by law, the state has used most of this revenue for healthcare, health education, substance abuse prevention and treatment, and law enforcement. In Colorado, about 30% of marijuana tax revenue is not earmarked and, therefore, lawmakers have the chance to negotiate where it will be spent.[14]

CANNABIS AND BEER: LEARNING FROM THE PAST

In addition to being home to one of the first legal recreational marijuana markets in the US, Colorado is also home to the headquarters of the American Homebrewers Association and the Brewers Association. Interestingly, American homebrewers were some of the first innovators to experiment with marijuana beers (Rosenthal 1996, 4). These early adopters were most likely aware of the illegality of marijuana but forged ahead with putting it into small-batch homebrews, showing that beers containing active THC can be made successfully.

In contrast to homebrewers, commercial craft brewers can only operate if they have a brewing permit issued by the Alcohol and Tobacco Tax and Trade Bureau (TTB), an agency of the Department of the Treasury, and so are very aware that they could lose their permit and livelihood if they brew with anything that is illegal under federal law. However, this is not to insinuate that today's craft brewers are standing by idle, waiting for federal legalization. Although this topic will be covered in other chapters, many craft breweries have either produced beers with cannabis terpenes to mimic the smell of marijuana (e.g., Hemperor Pale Ale by New Belgium Brewing Company), brewed with CBD (e.g., George Washington's Secret Stash by Dad's and Dude's Breweria), or produced non-alcoholic beers with psychoactive THC (e.g., Grainwave by CERIA Brewing Company).

It should be noted that non-alcoholic beers avoid excess federal scrutiny by not having alcohol, which allows brewers to experiment with cannabis in a limited way. Craft brewers have pioneered efforts in this area and will continue to forge new paths as more and more states move to fully legalize marijuana. However, it is necessary to provide a warning in regard to combining cannabinoids with alcohol at any concentration. The functionality of cannabinoids will be discussed further in chapter 5, but it is enough to note here that it is very clear cannabinoids cause known and unknown reactions in the human body. For example, THC will lead to intoxication; whereas CBD will lead to the calming of nausea and is used in the treatment of seizures in children with severe forms of epilepsy. Numerous other cannabinoids also cause reactions, independently or in conjunction with the effects of THC and CBD.

---

[14] Jesse Paul, "Where does Colorado's marijuana tax money go? The state made a flow chart to answer the $1 billion question," *Colorado Sun*, June 12, 2019, 2:42 p.m. MDT, https://coloradosun.com/2019/06/12/where-does-colorados-marijuana-tax-money-go/.

Since conclusive proof does not yet exist as to the actions and interactions of all of the cannabinoids in marijuana, brewers with interest in this area should keep in mind an event in the not too distant past where beverage manufacturers combined alcoholic beverages with caffeine. In 1999, when young people were experimenting with ways to keep the party going all night, they found that caffeinated energy drinks worked well when mixed with spirits, such as vodka, allowing them to stay buzzed without going to sleep.[15] Soon after, brewers started to create "energy beers," which were simply ready-to-drink energy drinks with alcohol. The most popular among these was Four Loko, which, by 2008, came packaged in 24-ounce cans that "contained the equivalent of two Red Bulls and four normal beers."[16] As these powerful drinks became more popular, the press reported an alarming increase in blackouts and date rapes, and also hospitalizations caused by potentially lethal blood alcohol levels. Eventually, the US Food and Drug Administration publicly clarified that alcoholic beverages with added caffeine are a public health concern and should be removed from the market.

---

[15] Nickolaus Hines, "How To Make A Red Bull Vodka, According To The Bar That Invented It," Thrillist, July 25, 2018, https://www.thrillist.com/culture/how-to-make-red-bull-vodka-original-bar.

[16] Jay Cheshes, "Meet The Frat Boys Behind Four Loko, America's Most Hated Beer," The Fix, April, 21, 2011, https://www.thefix.com/content/four-loko.

2

PLANT BIOLOGY

CANNABIS TAXONOMY

There are many names that refer to the plant that can be used for sustainably making biofuel and paper, and for getting people intoxicated. Names such as pot, weed, dope, reefer, etc., all refer to the cannabis plant. Originally classified by Swedish botanist Carl Linnaeus in 1753, *Cannabis* is a genus of erect herbs in the family Cannabaceae, a botanical family of flowering plants. A complete scientific plant name often ends with some identifier relating to the person responsible for specifying the epithet of a species. These identifiers are typically abbreviated, with species named by Linnaeus himself having an "L.," hence, *Cannabis sativa* L.

Although still debated among botanists, at least 13 species or subspecies of *Cannabis* have been identified, with all being considered either varieties of

Naming Cannabis: Botanists versus Budtenders

Today's cannabis vernacular appears very straightforward and is usually reinforced by seemingly knowledgeable budtenders who give recommendations for "Sativa," "Indica," or hybrid strains. However, research has shown that these modern vernacular names for cannabis strains have been wrongly assigned over the years, with the result that today's strains do not align with the botanical classification of *Cannabis sativa* L. varieties (McPartland 2017, 117). Chemical fingerprinting and genetic analysis has shown that cannabis varieties can be properly identified as follows:

- The "Indica" strain, with short stature and broad leaflets, actually originated in the Afghan region and should be correctly labeled as *C. sativa* var. *afghanica*.
- The "Sativa" strain, with tall stature and narrow leaflets, originated in the Indian region and includes descendants in southeast Asia, Africa, and the Americas, and should be correctly labeled as *C. sativa* var. *indica*.
- The "Ruderalis" strain, is usually *C. sativa* var. *sativa*.

All three are varieties of one species, *C. sativa* L. Extensive cross-breeding has virtually erased the classical differences between "Indica" and "Sativa," and so chemical fingerprinting (i.e., testing for cannabinoid and terpene content) is required for true differentiation.

Cannabis sativa L.,[1] or three unique species identified as *C. sativa*, *C. indica*, and *C. ruderalis* (Hillig 2005). It should be noted that the naming of strains in the marijuana trade do not necessarily align with botanical nomenclature (see sidebar). The "Ruderalis" strain, with its low levels of THC, is important in the marijuana community mainly for its short life cycle and autoflowering ability, which make it useful to breed with other potent and flavorful strains of cannabis.[2] "*Sativa*," actually *C. indica*, is generally a tall plant with narrow leaves that grows well in warmer climates and can have high levels of THC.[3] "Indica," actually *C. sativa* var. *afghanica*, is shorter and has wider leaves than "Sativa," and grows well in cooler, higher-altitude environments (McPartland 2017).

Many beer and cannabis aficionados often refer to the hop plant and the cannabis plant as "cousins." This is because both plants are members of Cannabaceae (fig. 2.1). This family consists of 10 genera, each having at least one species in its particular grouping (McPartland 2018). *Cannabis* and *Humulus* (hop plants) are

---

[1]   International Plant Names Index (s.v. "Cannabis," filter for "specific," "generic"), https://ipni.org/?f=%2Cf_specific%2Cf_generic&q=Cannabis.

[2]   Will Hyde, "What Is Cannabis Ruderalis?" Leafly, June 4, 2015, https://www.leafly.com/news/cannabis-101/what-is-cannabis-ruderalis.

[3]   "*Cannabis sativa* L.," NewCROP, Center for New Crops & Plant Products, Purdue University, July 3, 1996, https://hort.purdue.edu/newcrop/duke_energy/Cannabis_sativa.html.

two of those genera. Species in both are dioecious herbs, meaning that there are male and female versions of the plant producing distinct male or female flowers. Only the female plants of both genera are grown commercially and valued for their flowers, while the males are either discarded or used for breeding purposes to create better varieties. However, there are a number of differences between hop and cannabis plants. Cannabis is an erect herb that grows straight up and does not require support. The hop plant is a twining vine that has a tendency to spiral around any supportive structure as it grows upward. Additionally, the types of flowers that each produces and the growing seasons (annual versus perennial) are other differences, which I will discuss further below.

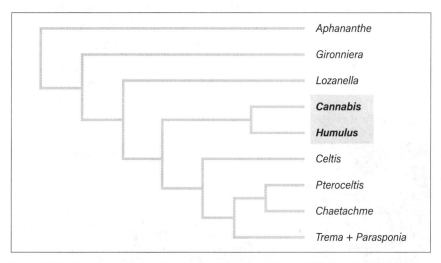

Figure 2.1. The Cannabaceae family of flowering plants, based on McPartland (2018) and Yang et al. (2013).

STRUCTURE AND GROWTH: *HUMULUS* VERSUS *CANNABIS*

The saying that cannabis and hops are cousins can be inferred by looking at their proximity within the Cannabaceae family tree, but it probably also evolved from a commonly held belief that the two plants could be fused together (grafted) to create a hop plant with THC, or a cannabis plant with hop components. Surprisingly, this was not an urban legend. In 1975 botanical researchers published a scientific paper in which they grafted the two plants together successfully. Although the grafted plants demonstrated healthy growth, the researchers reported that there was no evidence that cannabinoid production crossed over from the cannabis graft to the hop plant, or vice versa (Crombie and Crombie 1975). Although grafting did not produce multifunctional plants in 1975, modern methods of gene cloning could be capable of introducing the gene for cannabinoid production into the hop plant to grow hops with THC (Carvalho et al. 2017). This is relevant because the biosynthetic pathway for cannabinoid production has been identified and the genes in this pathway are available for researchers to employ in unique ways, such as using microorganisms to biosynthesize cannabinoids. Scientists have recently put the appropriate genes into yeast cells to produce THC and CBD (Luo et al. 2019). It is only a matter of time before these cannabis genes are cloned into hop plants.

Humulus (Hops)

People who hear about the connection between hops and cannabis are sometimes puzzled because, aside from both being green, the plants look quite distinct (fig. 2.2), especially with the large, unique fan leaves that grow on cannabis plants versus the rather ordinary leaves seen on hops (fig. 2.3). Hop plants emerge from the ground as strongly growing vines, also called bines. Modern hop yards use structural supports known as trellises, around which the hop plants twist in a clockwise direction as they climb upward using hooked hairs to grip onto surfaces. This framework of supports and twine allows the plants to grow to as much as 30 feet per season (just over 9 meters).

Figure 2.2. Comparison of hop plants growing on trellises (*left*), and cannabis plants growing in a grow house (*right*). © Getty/*Aaron007 (left); FatCamera (right)*.

Figure 2.3. Comparison of hop leaves (*left*) with uniquely shaped marijuana fan leaf (*right*). © Getty/*Ellen11 (left); George Peters (right)*.

This rapid growth has always been known to hop growers and appreciated by hobbyists who grow them, but was also noted by Charles Darwin, who reported the tip of a hop plant grew so fast that it completed a full circle of twining growth within two hours as he lay watching from his sickbed (Neve 1991, 1). After the growing season ends, the hops are harvested and the bines cut down; the shorter days and cold weather signal the plant to die down to the ground level. However, the roots remain alive but dormant in the soil, with the main portion, known as the crown, storing nutrients and preparing to repeat its impressive growth cycle the next year. Extensions of the plant grow under the soil horizontally and are referred to as rhizomes, which have buds that can grow upward to grow into new stems and foliage. Hop growers routinely harvest rhizomes and propagate new hop plants by planting the rhizomes as desired. Home gardeners find out quickly that hop plants should be grown in isolated containers to limit the spread of unwanted growth throughout their garden via rhizomes.

Cannabis

Cannabis plants, unlike hops, are hardy plants that grow upright without the need for a supporting structure. Whether in the wild or in domesticated grow houses, "Sativa" plants can grow up to 20 feet (6 meters) each growing season, while "Indica" can grow up to about six feet per season (almost two meters). Of course, modern grow houses strive to limit the height and maximize the production of buds per plant by using various trimming and pruning methods.

Cannabis plants found in nature are annual plants, meaning that at the end of the growing season the plant dies and a new plant emerges from seed the next year. Cannabis naturally produces seeds each growing season, which have an approximate 50:50 chance of resulting in male or female plants. As mentioned previously, female plants are more desirable than males because of the growth of buds and the high amount of terpenes and cannabinoids they produce, especially THC.

Male plants are discarded to prevent the female plants from being pol-linated and using up valuable resources to make seeds instead of focusing growth on buds. In other words, the presence of male plants can result in the loss of millions of dollars of valuable cannabis products. Therefore, it is critical that growers identify male and female plants. Generally, when a plant is about six weeks old, it will display female or male growths at the nodes where the leaves attach to the stem. Males will display small pollen sacs that are rounded, spade-shaped structures. Females will develop pistils encapsulated by bracts in the nodes that display long hair-like structures (fig. 2.4).

Figure 2.4. Male (*left*) and female versions of the cannabis plant. The pollen sacs of the male on the left are in contrast to the hair-like pistil of the female on the right. © *Getty/ Ava-Leigh (left); Joe Giampaoli (right).*

Rather than take a 50:50 chance of the new cannabis plants being male, modern cannabis growers use techniques to force plants to produce seeds that will turn into primarily female plants. One technique to force seeds to produce female plants involves applying solutions of microscopic silver particles to force them to produce pollen in a similar way that a male plant produces it. The female pollen then pollinates female plants, producing seeds that genetically will be virtually 100% female since both parents were female.[4] (There is always a slim chance that a genetically male seed will be among them.) These resulting seeds are referred to as feminized seeds.

Further, modern, professional growing operations are able to keep female plants alive at the end of the growing season using various nutrients and light exposure techniques to trick them into restarting the vegetative phase of growth after harvesting. Not only does this keep them productive for many years, these long-lived, female "mother" plants can then be cloned by clipping off a sturdy branch and planting it with root hormones to encourage root growth. This type of cloning is used quite often by growers who wish to propagate a certain mother plant that exhibits favorable characteristics.

FLOWERS OF *HUMULUS* AND *CANNABIS*

Hop Cones

Although similar in some ways, the flowers that the female hop and cannabis plants produce look very different (fig. 2.5). A hop flower, usually called a hop cone, or strobile, resembles a pinecone but with a soft, springy

---

[4]   Kannabia Seed Company, "What Are Feminized Cannabis Seeds?" Leafly, February 21, 2018, https://www.leafly.com/news/growing/what-are-feminized-cannabis-seeds.

feel. Hop cones are light green to green when fully ripened, and are often grouped into clumps that hang from the branches of the hop plant. The flowers are soft to the touch and fragrant.

When a hop cone is sliced open it reveals a structure consisting of four parts, the strig, bracts, bracteoles, and lupulin glands (Neve 1991, 2–7). The strig is the central axis of the hop cone to which the leafy structures attach. The bracts consist of the outer leaves on the hop cone and are attached to the strig and have almost no lupulin. Bracts are very rich in polyphenol compounds. The bracteoles are the inner leaf structures that are supported by the bract. The fourth and most important part are the lupulin glands, which are underneath the bracteoles (fig. 2.6). The lupulin glands are bright yellow in color because of lupulin powder, which contains the aromatic oils and flavoring components that give beer its bitter taste when brewed. Besides being highly fragrant, lupulin powder is very oily and sticky. Similar to the concentration of cannabis trichomes (described later), lupulin powder can be concentrated and used in the brewing process to make extremely aromatic and flavorful beers.

Figure 2.5. Comparison of hop cones (*left*) and cannabis colas (*right*). © Getty/*David Gomez (left); rgbspace (right)*.

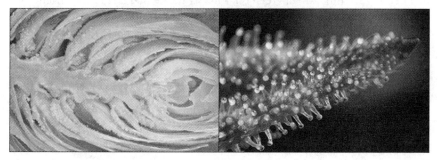

Figure 2.6. Comparison of hop cone lupulin glands (*left*) and cannabis trichomes (*right*), both magnified views. © Getty/*matzaball (left); Gleti (right)*.

Cannabis Buds

Unlike the hanging cones of hops, the flowers, or buds, of a female cannabis plant grow at the tips of stems, which are called bud sites. The main stem bud site is called the cola. So, although a "cannabis cola" may bring to mind images of a tall, green can of weed-flavored soda, it actually refers to the tip of the main stem where buds will form. Cannabis plants growing naturally usually have one large cola at the highest point (the main stem) of the plant, with smaller bud sites appearing at the ends of minor stems. Cannabis plants grown commercially undergo pruning and trimming routines that encourage the plant to form more main stems with colas than usual and, therefore, markedly improve the yield.

Cannabis buds can be green or blue-greenish in color, and before trimming have numerous distinctive appendages growing out from different areas around the bud (fig. 2.7). Brightly colored structures seen on buds are called stigma, which emanate from the female sexual organs called pistils and are hair-like growths for collecting male pollen. Stigmas start out white in color and then change to bright orange, yellow, red, green, or purple when the plant is mature and ready for harvest.

In cannabis buds, the hairlike stigma grow from the pistils. The pistils are found within small structures called calyxes. Calyxes protect the female reproductive organs and are densely covered with glandular trichomes, which are bulb-shaped structures on the surface and rich in cannabinoids and essential oils.[5] Cannabis buds also have bracts and bracteoles, similar to hops, and the bracts have been misidentified as calyxes.[6] In essence, this view is that the pistil emerges from the cells of the calyx and that this structure is surrounded by the bracteole, which in turn is protected by the bract. Regardless of which point of view is correct, it is obvious to see that the stigma from a growing cannabis plant emerges from a small green bulbous structure that is rich with trichomes and serves as a support for the pistil. It is also clear that the abundance of glandular trichomes means this structure is desirable as a rich source of cannabinoids and terpenes.

If pollen were to be collected by the pistils, it would result in fertilization and the female plant using its resources to produce seeds instead of

---

[5] "Getting To Know The Cannabis Calyx, Resinous To The Top," *Cannabis Blog*, Royal Queen Seeds, November 16, 2019, https://www.royalqueenseeds.com/blog-getting-to-know-the-cannabis -calyx-resinous-to-the-top-n414.

[6] Mel Frank, "The Cannabis Female Flower," O'Shaughnessy's Online, original article in *O'Shaughnessy's* (Winter 2018/19), accessed November 30, 2020, https://beyondthc.com/the-cannabis-female-flower/.

flavorful, potent flowers/buds. This is a constant threat when growing out-doors because pollen is airborne and can travel long distances. Grow houses are strictly controlled and minimize the presence of pollen, with workers even using foot baths and laboratory gowns to provide protection. Pistils do not contain significant amounts of cannabinoids and so are not highly sought after, but they are kept during the trimming process and combined with other trimmed parts.

Besides pistils, buds usually have small protruding leaf-like structures that are densely filled with trichomes, commonly referred to as "sugar leaves." These leaves are smaller and different compared to the characteristic and well-known fan leaves seen on the stems of the plant. The numerous trichomes on the sugar leaves give an appearance similar to sugar crystals coating the leaves, hence the name.

Sometimes buds that are trimmed are referred to as "nugs," which gives consumers a clear distinction between a fully manicured bud for sale in a dispensary and a bud growing on a mature plant. Nugs usually have a small segment of the stem, which is referred to as the tail (fig. 2.7, *right*).

Figure 2.7. Untrimmed cannabis bud (*left*) and a trimmed cannabis bud (*right*). Orange colored stigma and sugar leaves are present on the untrimmed bud. The trimmed bud, also called a nug, displays the stem, or tail. © Getty/*Seastock (left); Belterz (right)*.

Cannabis "Trim"

During the trimming process, sugar leaves are trimmed to give the bud its desirable, ovoid shape (fig. 2.7). As rich as the sugar leaves appear, they result in a harsh taste when smoked and so they are usually collected and used for other purposes, such as making hash or edibles. In fact, all of the excess plant materials that are trimmed off of buds and the plant are referred to as "trim" and are useful for cannabinoid extraction, or even for juicing or using as herbs on certain dishes such as pizza when the munchies strike.*

* "What to Do with Cannabis Trim: 10 Tricks to Turn Waste Into Big Profit," Grow Light Central, accessed November 30, 2020, https://growlightcentral.com/blogs/news/what-to-do-with-cannabis-trim.

EVALUATING CONES AND BUDS

The qualitative evaluation of hops usually involves a hand-rub test, where a person places a few hop cones between their hands and rubs vigorously in a circular motion to break apart the hops and the lupulin glands. Once their hands are sticky with hop resin, the person brings their hands up to their nose and sniffs to evaluate the various aromas that have been released. Since myrcene has a high concentration in fresh hops, an herbal, musky note is almost always the predominant aroma. Finally, quantitative chemical analysis will show the potential bittering ability of the hop and provide a measure of the oils that will contribute flavor and aroma to the final beer.

In the world of cannabis the term "hand rubbing" exists but usually refers to the ancient method of making hashish by forming small blocks or disks of compressed, concentrated trichomes with the hands. This method of concentrating trichomes results in a product that is very aromatic and flavorful and has very strong psychoactive effects. The usual way of evaluating cannabis is by inspecting the buds visually and nasally. Buds should be green in color with streaks of white, yellow, or red. Any stark discoloration can be a sign of mold or pest damage. Brown coloration can be a sign of aging and oxidation. The aroma should be fragrant and representative of the variety. Chemical analysis will show the percentage of THC, CBD, and other cannabinoids, and also which terpenes are present. The terpenes will determine the qualitative aroma and can include descriptors such as herbal, grassy, fruity, floral, or spice-like. Quite often, the particular combination of terpenes will determine the name of the cultivar, such as the 'Pineapple Express', 'Banana OG', and 'Super Lemon Haze'. Buds can also be described as "skunky," but that is usually reserved for lower-quality cannabis.

Interestingly, both hops and cannabis require heat to transform some of their components into their "active" forms. Alpha acids in hop cones are the primary source of bitterness in beer. However, these alpha acids are precursor compounds—they must be heated, usually to boiling, to be converted into isomerized alpha acids, which are the actual compounds that provide the bitter taste in beer. Similarly in cannabis, the main compound that provides the feeling of intoxication is THC, but it exists in the form of tetrahydrocannabinolic acid (THCA) in buds and plant materials. THCA must be heated to over 212°F (100°C) in order to be decarboxylated and converted to THC.

3

AGRONOMY

With the legalization of hemp via the Agriculture Improvement Act of 2018, many farmers began growing hemp as a commodity to be used for fiber, food products, and other industrial uses. These farmers found that maximizing hemp growth and yields involved a similar approach to that for other agricultural commodities. The application of water, fertilizer, and sunlight resulted in healthy, robust hemp plants. In contrast, growing high-quality marijuana year-round in greenhouses takes more thought and care to ensure the optimal production of terpenes and cannabinoids, especially THC.

Before getting started, anyone wanting to grow cannabis for THC-containing marijuana should first check local laws to make sure that this is legal in their locale. If there is any doubt, then legal advice should be obtained. Growing cannabis involves having thorough and up-to-date knowledge of local laws, even where recreational marijuana is state legal. For examples of how laws can differ from state to state, see chapter 6. It should also be stressed that some laws treat the production of hemp and marijuana differently. This is important because some regulations may be present for hemp but not for marijuana, and vice versa. Growers can never be too careful regarding the law.

After determining the legal situation, the first decision to make when growing marijuana at home is the strain. As noted previously, "Indica" strains are generally regarded as strains that provide an intoxicated feeling throughout the body (i.e., a "body high"), while "Sativa" strains provide a more focused intoxication in the head or mind. (See p. 22 for an explanation of strains and botanical varieties.) Research has proposed that "Indica" originated in central Asia (Clarke and Watson 2007, 8–9) and from this location it can be presumed that optimal outdoor growth occurs from the 30th parallel north up to the 50th parallel north. In North America, this would be from as far south as Houston, Texas, to as far north as Vancouver, British Columbia. Across the Atlantic, this would be from as far south as Cairo, Egypt to as far north as Brussels, Belgium. And, since seasons are opposite on the other side of the equator, optimal growth for "Indica" strains should also be expected from the 30th parallel south down to the 50th parallel south. In contrast, "Sativa" plants are thought to have originated in the areas of Thailand and Mexico, and so are thought to grow optimally outdoors between the 30th parallel north and the 30th parallel south.[1] Outdoor growing, if legal, can take advantage of the natural conditions of these growing areas and favor either "Sativa" or "Indica," but modern indoor growing techniques that use light, temperature, and humidity control can mimic these areas to grow "Sativa" and "Indica" plants anywhere in the world. Hybrids of "Indica" and "Sativa" can also be expected to grow anywhere when conditions are controlled for light exposure, temperature, and humidity.

Know Before You Grow

It bears repeating that local laws should be observed. Some states strictly allow only indoor growing in an area that is secured from children. Be sure to check into the legality of growing in your local area.

LIFE STAGES OF CANNABIS

When growing cannabis, it is important to know the four stages of the life cycle of the plant so that nutrients can be applied appropriately to maximize production of desirable compounds, especially terpenes and THC. These

---

[1] "How to choose the right kind of strain for your climate," Marijuana Grow Guide, AMS [Amsterdam Marijuana Seeds], accessed November 30, 2020, https://amsterdammarijuanaseeds.com /grow-guide#choosing.

four stages usually take place during the 4–8 month growing cycle of most cannabis strains. The four stages are (1) germination, (2) seedling, (3) vegetative, and (4) flowering.[2]

Germination Stage

Germination is when a cannabis seed begins to sprout after exposure to water (fig. 3.1). In essence, water tends to "wake up" the seed from dormancy and begin the growth process. Soon after waking up, the seed sprouts a single root and then two leaves grow from the stem; at this stage, the seed is now a seedling. The two initial leaves are referred to as cotyledons. Germination generally lasts one to one and a half weeks. Seed packs of 5 or 10 seeds are readily available on the internet for prices ranging from US$40 to over $100. Again, check your local laws before ordering cannabis seeds online. Since female plants are the ones with desirable characteristics, many growers choose to skip seeds and purchase known clones from established growers, rather than starting seeds and then discovering that some or all of the plants are male.

Figure 3.1. Cannabis germination showing the plant emerging from the shell seed. © *Getty/Yarygin*.

---

[2]   Trevor Hennings, "Stages of the Marijuana Plant Growth Cycle," Leafly, January 17, 2020, https://www.leafly.com/news/growing/marijuana-plant-growth-stages.

Seedling Stage

The seedling stage (fig. 3.2) involves growth to the point where the plant has up to eight leaves and requires adequate light, heat, and moisture. This stage lasts two to four weeks, depending on the strain, and by the end the plant has bright green leaves that have the iconic marijuana leaf appearance. Many dispensaries sell cloned seedlings to legal residents of their respective states. Growing plants from seedlings can be much easier and faster than starting from seeds. Seedlings are also called "clones" since they are cloned from pure strains of female cannabis plants

Figure 3.2. Cannabis seedling showing the original cotyledons and two early leaves. © Getty/Dharmapada Behera.

and typically cost from US$20 to $40 or more. Customers who want to purchase clones at dispensaries are usually required to provide proof that they are residents of the state where the dispensary is located. Non-residents are generally denied any purchases of clones. However, if a dispensary sells a clone to a non-resident, then that purchaser should contemplate the very real legal consequences (fines and jail time) if caught.

Vegetative Stage

The vegetative stage, which can last one to four months, is when the plant begins to grow vigorously (fig. 3.3). At this point the plant requires up to 18 hours of light per day and a nutritious soil. This stage is when the plant becomes bushy as it grows leaves and stems; it is also when a plant starts to display whether it is male or female. Male plants should be destroyed or isolated away from female plants, not only because male plants have lower concentrations

Figure 3.3. Cannabis plant at the vegetative stage. © Getty/underworld111.

of cannabinoids but also because males will pollinate females, producing a crop with seeds. Seedless crops are the best crops from a quality perspective because the plant will focus energy and nutrients on growth instead of seed production. Male plants can be identified by looking for the pre-flowers that form at the "Y" where the stems meet the main stalk. The pre-flowers on a male plant are green and almond shaped, while the pre-flowers on a female plant are longer with string-like stigma protruding (fig. 3.4). The appearance of flowers marks the end of the vegetative stage.

Did you know?

The Spanish term *sin semilla* means without seed, or seedless. Over time, many people have mistakenly believed that "Sensimilla" is a potent strain of marijuana, but it really refers to a female plant that has not been fertilized by a male to produce seeds.

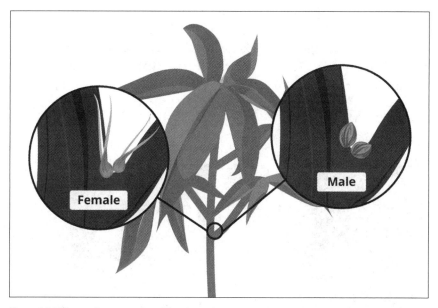

Figure 3.4. Difference between male and female pre-flowers on cannabis plants. *Image courtesy of Leafly.com.*

Flowering Stage

The flowering stage of cannabis (fig. 3.5) is triggered by the end of the growing season, when days get shorter and daylight hours decrease to less than 12 hours.

Lighting Grow Houses

Modern cannabis grow houses utilize specialized lighting (and appropriate humidity levels) in different rooms to simulate different phases of the growing season, in order to optimize growth during the four life stages. Plants are usually on wheeled carts that are moved from one lighted area to the next as the plants mature. Eye protection is generally required for anyone entering the intensely lit rooms. The ultimate goal is high quality, maximal cannabinoid and terpene production by the plants.

This stage is when buds form on the plants and cannabinoids begin to concentrate in the glandular trichomes. The plant is also trimmed at this stage in order to beautify the buds and maximize growth. Flowering can last 8 to 10 weeks. When the trichomes on the buds and on the plant change appearance from clear to cloudy, it is a sure sign that the flowering stage has ended and harvesting should begin (fig. 3.6). When trichomes turn from cloudy to amber in color this is a sign that THC is degrading to cannabinol (CBN) and that the quality of the harvest could be at risk if harvesting is postponed any longer.

Figure 3.5. Cannabis plant at the flowering stage with buds that have not been trimmed. © Getty/ Yarygin.

Figure 3.6. Trichomes, both clear and cloudy, on a mature cannabis plant that is ready for harvest. © Getty/Gleti.

GROWING CONDITIONS

Nutritional Requirements

As the cannabis plant passes through each life cycle, maintaining the correct level of nutrients is critical for maximum cannabinoid production of the highest quality.

Nutrient fertilizers are generally not recommended for young seedlings as they may lead to burning of the delicate tissues, much like happens when you overfertilize a lawn. However, when the seedling has developed three to four sets of leaves then light fertilization can begin using a combination of nitrogen, phosphorous, and potassium, often abbreviated as NPK following their respective chemical symbols. The best ratio of NPK is N-11, P-40, K-13 (11:40:13) for seedlings. (These ratios are listed on most commercially available plant fertilizers, as are recommended application rates. For example, some Miracle-Gro branded fertilizers have an application rate of ½ tsp per gallon of water.)

The vegetative state is when vigorous growth takes place and therefore requires more nutrients for healthy growth. An NPK ratio of 19:5:20 will set the stage for future development of flowers and buds. Fertilizers with higher amounts of nitrogen should be avoided since it has been reported that these types can result in marijuana with a strong metallic taste.[3]

The flowering stage requires less nitrogen and more potassium and phosphorous to encourage the growth of buds with high levels of cannabinoids. An NPK ratio of 15:6:30 is recommended for flowering plants. During the late bloom phase, the plant will need plenty of phosphorous and potassium for healthy buds and the need for nitrogen will decrease drastically. Accordingly, an NPK ratio of 0:27:27 will favor the production of buds with good levels of cannabinoids.

Table 3.1 Recommended fertilizer NPK ratio for each stage of cannabis growth

Life cycle stage	Recommended NPK ratio
Seedling	11:40:13
Vegetative	19:5:20
Flowering	15:6:30
Late Bloom	0:27:27

---

[3] "7 Marijuana Growing Tips Every Grower Needs to Know," Recreational Marijuana News, *420 Intel*, August 20, 2020, https://420intel.com/articles/2020/08/20/7-marijuana-growing-tips-every-grower-needs-know.

Soil Requirements

High-quality soil is also critical for producing high-quality marijuana. Poor-quality soil can contain microbes that are detrimental to young marijuana plants. Further, overfertilized soil can provide too many nutrients and result in fertilizer burn and contamination of the soil with heavy metals. The best soil should contain minimal nutrients, since those will be controlled by the grower, and it should provide good drainage.

A grower can purchase prepackaged soil or prepare it at home. Good soil should have a pH between 6 and 7 to allow for optimal uptake of nutrients. If the soil does not have good drainage, additions of perlite, sand, or compost can improve the soil dramatically. Poor drainage can lead to water retention in the soil and cause the plant root structures to rot.

Growing Containers

Containers for growing marijuana plants can range from plastic to clay and even include fabric growing bags. As long as water can drain out, almost any container will work so long as the container does not leach any toxins into the soil. In general, seedlings can be grown successfully in 12–16 fl. oz. (350–500 mL) clear plastic disposable drinking cups with drain holes in the bottom. The small size allows complete control of nutrients and the ability to pick up the container when inspecting for pests or any other issues. At the end of the seedling stage, when the plant is 3–4 inches tall (8–10 cm), it can be transplanted to a 3- or 5-gallon pot (11–20 L) to give the roots room to grow. The plant can stay in this pot until harvest or it can be transplanted to a larger pot to allow for fuller growth.

Cannabis can be grown in a well maintained, backyard garden successfully. However, local laws should be observed since some states strictly allow only indoor growing in an area that is secured from children.

Light Requirements

Recalling that cannabis originated in regions of the planet with abundant, natural sunlight, any attempts to grow indoors should try to recreate that light spectrum. Due to the enormous diversity among cannabis strains, each strain has its own optimum light requirements. There are many types of artificial light on the market, but only a few types of grow lights result in high-quality cannabis plants: LED, fluorescent, metal halide, and high-pressure sodium.[4]

---

[4]   Max Anderson, "How to Select the Best Grow Lights for Your Marijuana Grow," *How to Grow Weed: Beginner's Guide to Growing in 2020*, Production Grower, December 17, 2019, https://productiongrower.com/blogs/how-to-grow-weed/selecting-grow-lights.

Any one of these light sources can be used for the entirety of the growing cycle, but when used in the right sequence according to the plant's life cycle, high-quality marijuana can be harvested season after season by professional growers.

Seedlings grow best when exposed to the purple-white light emitted by compact fluorescent lights (CFLs). While CFLs are adequate for smaller grows, larger T5 fluorescent grow lights are best for larger grows. Lighting should be as close to the seedlings as possible without burning them. Fans may be required for adequate cooling and ventilation.

When seedlings mature into the vegetative state, more intense lighting in the blue spectrum is required to maximize yields. This can be accomplished by using metal halide lights for up to 18 hours per day to simulate peak summer days. Timers should be used to control the hours of light to which the plants are exposed. Fans are required due to the heat output from metal halide lights. Again, proximity to the light without burning is important.

As the plants enter the flowering stage, a full-spectrum/yellow light is required for the best yield and this usually requires high-pressure sodium lights for up to 12 hours per day to simulate daylight during late summer. Fans and ventilation are required due to the heat output from this type of light source.

Temperature and Humidity

During growing season, temperature and humidity should be closely watched and controlled to help ensure the highest quality marijuana. Growers often simulate the seasons to be able to have a constant supply available. Good quality thermometers and hygrometers should be used to monitor conditions, as adjustments and interventions are often required to maintain optimum conditions.

When plants are young, the seedlings' roots will not be fully grown and able to bring in moisture. Therefore, a humidity level of 65%–70% should be maintained until the vegetative state is reached.[5] Seedlings also normally appear in the spring and so will mature best when held at a temperature of 68–77°F (20–25°C).

As the plants enter the vegetative state, summertime would normally be starting. A humidity level from 70% down to 40% will keep the plants from getting too dry, especially since the roots will be wicking up moisture from the soil. To simulate summer growing conditions, plants should be kept at 72–82°F (22–28°C) to ensure optimal growth.

----

5 "Indoor Cannabis Growing," *Growing Cannabis*, Royal Queen Seeds, March 31, 2020, https://www.royalqueenseeds.com/blog-indoor-cannabis-growing-relative-humidity-and-temperatures-n243.

When flowers appear on the plants the humidity should be decreased to 40%–50%. The temperature should be decreased slightly to 68–79°F (20–26°C) so that the flowers can grow and mature quickly. When the buds are fully mature and close to harvesting, the humidity should be decreased to 30%–40% for the highest quality. Also, the temperature should be cooled to 64–75°F (18–24°C) to keep the buds in peak condition.

Table 3.2 A generalized growing regimen for two different cannabis strains

	Seedling stage →	Vegetative stage →	Flowering stage
"Sativa"	Fertilization – light Light – medium amount Humidity – high Temperature – warmer	Fertilization – medium Light – high, intense Humidity – high Temperature – warmer	Fertilization – medium Light – high Humidity – low Temperature – warmer
"Indica"	Fertilization – light Light – medium amount Humidity – high Temperature – cooler	Fertilization – high Light – medium to high Humidity – low Temperature – cooler	Fertilization – medium Light – medium to high Humidity – low Temperature – cooler

PESTS

Depending on the geographic location and location within a residence, sooner or later pests of one kind or another will make their presence known on cannabis plants. The best defense is to use common sense and rely on procedures that are generally used in backyard vegetable gardens. If growing outdoors, larger herbivores such as deer may find the taste of young cannabis plants appealing—typical remedies such as fencing or hot pepper sprays will usually discourage them.

Whether indoors or outdoors, small pests can be difficult to diagnose and eliminate.[6] A couple of the most common pests are spider mites and aphids (fig. 3.7 and 3.8). Spider mites are usually too small to notice with the naked eye, but their webs become noticeable when strung out between stems and leaves on the plant. Small, white dots are also commonly seen on the plants where the mites have bitten into the leaves. Aphids are another common pest and usually appear as small light-green dots on the underside of leaves, although they can come in various colors from off-white to dark brown. When mature, aphids usually have dark bodies with wings, but can appear lighter in color. Getting rid of pests such as these involves utilizing safe methods similar to those used

------

[6]   Nebula Haze, "Aphids," Grow Weed Easy, accessed November 30, 2020, https://www.growweedeasy.com/cannabis-plant-problems/aphids.

when growing vegetables that will be consumed. Any methods using organic and/or natural ingredients should be employed, if possible. The Department of Pesticide Regulation for the state of California published a useful list of active ingredients that are allowed for pest management in cannabis growing operations (table 3.3).

A visit to the local nursery or a call to the local university agricultural extension office will be helpful. For example, the extension office of Colorado State University offers an "Ask an Expert" option where experts will provide suggestions to help with almost any gardening issue (https://extension.colostate.edu/).

Figure 3.7. Spider mite infestation where the stem meets the stalk. © *Getty/NNhering.*

Figure 3.8. Two aphids infecting the underside of a leaf. © *Getty/Henrik L.*

Table 3.3 Legal pest management practices for cannabis growers in California

Active ingredient	Pest or disease
Azadirachtin	Aphids, white flies, fungus gnats, leaf miners, cutworms
Bacillus amyloliquefaciens strain D747	Root and crown diseases, powdery mildew, *Botrytis*
Bacillus subtilis QST	Root diseases, powdery mildew
Bacillus thuringiensisa subsp. *kurstaki* subsp. *israelensis*	Moth larvae Fly larvae
Beauveria bassiana	Whiteflies, aphids, thrips
Burkholderia spp. strain A396	Mites, leafhoppers, aphids, whiteflies, thrips, moth larvae
Capsaicin	Mites, leafhoppers, whiteflies, thrips, moth larvae, repellent (insects & vertebrates)
Castor oil	Repellent (moles, voles, gophers)
Cinnamon, cinnamon oil	Slugs and snails, mites, leafhoppers, aphids, whiteflies, moth larvae
Citric acid	Bacteria, fungi, mites, insects
Cloves, clove oil	Bacteria, fungi
Corn oil	Fungi, mites, insects
Cottonseed oil	Fungi, mites, insects
Ferric sodium EDTA (see also iron phosphate)	Slugs and snails
Garlic, garlic oil	Mites, leafhoppers, aphids, whiteflies, moth larvae
Geraniol	Fungi, rodent repellent, mites, insects
Gliocladium virens[a]	Root diseases
Horticultural oils (refined petroleum oils)	Mites, aphids, whiteflies, thrips, powdery mildew
Insecticidal soaps (potassium salts of fatty acids)	Aphids, whiteflies, cutworms, budworms
Iron phosphate (see also ferric sodium EDTA)	Slugs and snails
Isaria fumosorosea	Mites, aphids, whiteflies, thrips
Neem oil	Mites, powdery mildew
Peppermint, peppermint oil	Bacteria, fungi, mites, leafhoppers, aphids, whiteflies, moth larvae
Potassium bicarbonate (see also sodium bicarb.)	Powdery mildew
Potassium silicate	Powdery mildew, mites, aphids
Potassium sorbate	Fungi, mites, insects

Active ingredient	Pest or disease
Predatory nematodes	Fungus gnats
Putrescent whole egg solids	Squirrel, rabbit, and deer repellent
Rosemary, rosemary oil	Bacteria, fungi, leafhoppers, aphids, whiteflies, moth larvae
Sesame, sesame oil	Mites, leafhoppers, aphids, whiteflies, moth larvae
Sodium bicarbonate (see also potassium bicarb.)	Powdery mildew
Sodium chloride	Minor active ingredient in some fungicide and insecticide formulations
Soybean oil	Mites, insects
Reynoutria sachalinensis extract	Powdery mildew
Sulfur	Mites, flea beetles
Trichoderma harzianum	Root diseases
Thyme oil	Mites, leafhoppers, aphids, whiteflies, moth larvae

Source: Department of Pesticide Regulation (2017).

Notes: The table lists active ingredients for pest and disease management that are exempt from residue tolerance requirements per the US Environmental Protection Agency; exempt from registration requirements under the Federal Insecticide, Fungicide, and Rodenticide Act, 7 U.S.C. §136 et seq. (1996); or registered for broad enough use to include use on cannabis.

[a] Also known as *Trichoderma virens*.

PRUNING AND HARVESTING

Pruning and harvesting of cannabis plants, or any plants that will be consumed by humans, should always involve good agricultural and manufacturing practices. Tools that come into contact with the plant should be well functioning and clean. Gloves should be worn, if necessary, and safety should always be top of mind.

When to Prune

Pruning of cannabis plants is not a necessity and the decision to do so is sometimes controversial. Many people allow the plants to grow naturally without pruning and then harvest all the parts that contain cannabinoids. Other people prune plants in the hopes of increasing bud and/or THC yields, often following the lead of professional growers who claim yield increases of up to 25%. If done improperly, pruning can lead to viral or bacterial infection, poor growth, or even plant death.

To raise the healthiest plants most new growers should avoid pruning, except when they notice leaves that are dying, as evidenced by them turning yellow or brown. In these cases, it is best to remove the dying leaves as soon as possible so that the plant does not waste energy providing nutrients to these areas. When removing leaves or stems it is best to use scissors or a sharp knife and never rip or tear with bare hands. As a sidenote, during the plant's early life stages these leaves that are removed contain very little THC, but in the mature stages they will contain trichomes with THC. So, it is a good idea to keep these mature leaves to combine with future harvests. Only after several successful seasons of growing should a grower consider pruning their plants. There are several pruning methods used by professional growers to encourage the most efficient growth and thereby increased yields of up to 25% THC and other cannabinoids (yield being milligrams cannabinoid per gram dry material).[7]

Topping. Topping involves trimming the plant stem immediately below the growing tip and above the internode. Topping encourages growth of multiple heads.

Fimming. Fimming involves trimming the new vegetative growth at the tip of a branch, which encourages multiple heads and bushier growth. It is difficult to trim precisely and so the name comes from the phrase "f*&%, I missed."

Lollipopping. Lollipopping involves removing all growth at the base of the plant that does not get adequate light exposure. This encourages the plant to focus on growth at future flower sites at the top of the plant where it gets light. The shape of the plant resembles that of a lollipop.

Harvest Time

When the plants are mature and fully budded, and trichomes appear both clear and cloudy, proper steps should be taken for harvesting, since this final step of the growing season also involves drying and curing.[8]

Harvesting can be a bit messy because the resin that is present on the plant is very sticky and will build up on cutting blade surfaces and hands. However, since the resin is high in THC, it can be collected and formed into hashish.

When harvesting it is best to cut branches rather than the entire plant so that they can be hung to dry with plenty of spacing (fig. 3.9). Care should be taken to avoid excessive movement or shaking of the flowers so as not to lose valuable trichomes. The branches should be placed gently into large, clean plastic tubs during

[7] Robert Bergman, "Pruning Marijuana Plants," I Love Growing Marijuana, accessed November 30, 2020, https://www.ilovegrowingmarijuana.com/pruning/.

[8] "How to Harvest Cannabis Plants," *Sensi Seeds Blog*, August 23, 2020, https://sensiseeds.com/en/blog/how-to-harvest-cannabis-plants/.

harvesting. After harvesting is complete, each branch should be tied with a piece of string in order to be hung upside down for drying. The buds can be removed from the branches and dried separately on a screen to improve air circulation, if desired.

Drying should take place in a dark, cool, dry place for optimum results. A plastic tray should be placed underneath the buds and branches to catch any leaves or trichomes that may fall. The best conditions to aim for are 45%–55% humidity and 65–75°F (18–24°C). Drying can take place outside of these conditions, but this may result in mold formation if too humid, or off-tastes if too hot and dry. The buds and branches should be allowed to thoroughly dry out for 10 to 14 days.[9]

Care should be taken to ensure that drying does not occur too quickly as this can slow down the decomposition of chlorophyll. Too much chlorophyll can lead to bitter tasting smoke with a "green" aftertaste. The length of drying time will also affect flavor, smokability, and THC potency. The composition of terpenes will change from a high concentration of myrcene to a high concentration of caryophyllene (see next section). Smokability and optimum burn rate will occur when the buds have about 8% humidity, while users wanting to vape the product should try for 12%–15% humidity for optimal vaping.

Finally, an extended drying time will cause THC to break down to CBN, which leads to a less potent high. In summary, a 10-day aging period will produce marijuana that is more potent with a fresh character, while a 14-day aging period will lead to marijuana with slightly less THC but a more complex flavor. Each grower will find the optimum aging time to give the best, personalized results. If not growing your own, it is important to work closely with your grower to find the optimum drying time to suit your brewing process.

Figure 3.9. Marijuana plants harvested and drying. © *Getty/South Agency.*

---

9   Ed Rosenthal, "Drying and Curing Cannabis: The Art of Enhancing Effect and Flavor," Ed Rosenthal.com, accessed November 30, 2020, https://www.edrosenthal.com/the-guru-of-ganja-blog/drying-and -curing-cannabis-the-art-of-enhancing-effect-and-flavor.

Curing

Curing is the "proper" way to age cannabis, and is the final step that follows harvesting and drying. Some believe it is critical to producing great-tasting, smokable material that can be pulled from storage. As an aside, some home growers avoid curing and enjoy smoking aged marijuana that is simply stored in sealed glass jars. Curing can be as simple as placing dried buds and flowers into clean wooden or cardboard boxes. Alternatively, dried buds and flowers can be gently put into plastic zip-tie bags with enough spacing to allow for plenty of air circulation; the plastic bags are then placed inside brown paper bags.

Whether boxed or bagged, the marijuana is allowed to cure for up to one week at 64°F (18°C) and 50% humidity. After this, the buds and leaves should be gently transferred to sealable glass jars. Again, allow enough spacing for good air circulation. The glass jars should be opened every day for inspection and to gently stir the buds and leaves for even curing. After a couple of days of curing in glass jars, the grower can begin sampling the buds. Curing can continue for several more weeks, or even months, but it all depends on personal taste. Many people enjoy buds when they are freshly cured, while others find more flavor and smokability after at least a month of curing.

A final note on curing marijuana is that the terpene content, and thereby the flavor and aroma, is greatly affected by curing (fig. 3.10). The aroma of freshly cut marijuana is high in myrcene (also found in hops), which has an

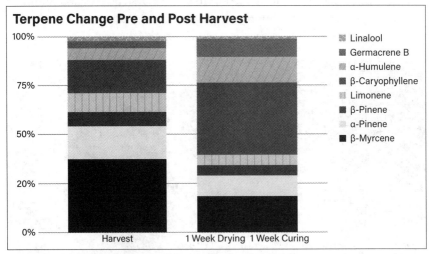

Figure 3.10. Change in terpene content at harvest versus 2 weeks post-harvest as measured by proprietary headspace technology. Plants were grown in "controlled conditions in a medical cannabis greenhouse." Information on strains and drying/harvesting conditions is not available. *Source: "Terpenes' qualitative change post cannabis drying and curing" conducted in September 2020. Courtesy of Eybna Technologies Ltd.*

herbal and citrus-like aroma. Many aficionados recognize and desire this component, and it helps explain why live resin and live vape products are some of the best sellers in many dispensaries.[10] However, after one week of drying and one week of curing, caryophyllene, which has a woody and spicy aroma, becomes the prominent terpene.

All harvested marijuana that has been properly prepared for smoking is suitable for using in brewing. As described in the recipes section (chapter 9), the marijuana can be placed in the beer aging tank to extract flavors and cannabinoids into the beer. Additionally, this same material can be extracted and then the extract can be infused into aging or finished beer.

Evaluation for Use in Brewing

The evaluation of marijuana by brewers who wish to use it for brewing is similar to the evaluation of hops. Aroma and appearance are critical.

The aroma of marijuana should be rich with terpenes. Dank, tropical, chocolate, and diesel-like are all indicators of varietal-specific terpenes. Lack of terpene-derived aroma indicates poor quality. A prominent grassy/hay-like aroma is indicative of improper curing or freshly harvested marijuana. Off-aromas, such as moldy, should not be present.

The appearance of marijuana should be rated for color and structure. First, the color should be a shade of green (very light to somewhat dark), and can have accents of purple, blue, or gold. If the buds appear brown, red, yellow, or white, it indicates poor quality and the product should be avoided. Second, the buds should be fairly tight and densely packed. Buds that are very loose with a visible stem indicate poorly grown plants that should be avoided. Buds should be neatly trimmed of excess leaf material and be covered with trichomes, giving a frosty appearance. Buds with excessive leaf material or with amber colored trichomes or no trichomes should be avoided. Any traces of fuzzy, white mold or of dead insects are not acceptable.

---

[10]   "Researchers Reveal How Curing Cannabis Impacts Overall Terpene Levels," Cannabis Technology News, *420 Intel*, October 13, 2020, https://420intel.com/articles/2020/10/13/researchers-reveal-how-curing-cannabis-impacts-overall-terpene-levels.

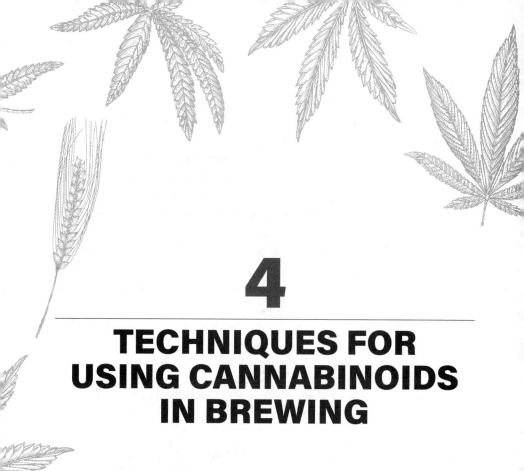

4

TECHNIQUES FOR USING CANNABINOIDS IN BREWING

This chapter will discuss the various strategies that brewers have explored to put cannabis into alcoholic and non-alcoholic brews. Since cannabidiol (CBD) is very similar to delta-9-tetrahydrocannabinol (THC) and other cannabinoids, and since alcoholic and non-alcoholic beverages are very similar and usually greater than 95% water, any methods described below *should* apply generally to CBD, THC, and/or many other cannabis phytocannabinoids used in a malt beverage. Additionally, beer is described below, but the beverage can be hard seltzer, non-alcoholic beer, or even sparkling water.

Cannabis remains illegal under federal law, and it is important to note that the addition of any cannabinoid to any kind of alcoholic beverage is illegal. At our brewery, CERIA Brewing Company, THC and CBD are dosed into non-alcoholic beer only and never into beer with alcohol. Other beverages for sale that contain CBD, where legal, are also non-alcoholic, usually sparkling or still flavored waters. Finally, consumers of cannabis beverages should avoid should avoid overconsumption at all times. Perhaps a friend or budtender suggests that 100 mg of CBD is optimal, or a popular TV personality suggests that 1 mg per pound of body weight is most effective. Taking advice from unproven sources should be avoided at all costs.

Prior to the passage of the Agriculture Improvement Act of 2018 (often referred to as the 2018 farm bill), in which hemp was removed from the Controlled Substances Act, professional brewers were very hesitant to consider brewing with hemp for fear of losing their federally issued brewer's permit. In contrast, homebrewers experimented with hemp and even posted recipes on websites for others to try to replicate. Some craft breweries made a name for themselves by naming beers after marijuana strains or after cannabis vocabulary, such as "420" Extra Pale Ale by Sweetwater Brewing Company in Georgia. However, none were daring enough to try brewing with hemp, even though hemp contains less than 0.3% dry weight of the psychoactive component, THC.

It should be noted that hemp seeds are specifically mentioned in the 2018 farm bill as a part of the hemp plant that can be harvested and sold in the food chain in the US because they do not contain cannabinoids; specifically, they do not contain THC or CBD.

Hemp Ale and Washington's Secret Stash

One of the first—and still existing—brewers to brew a beer with hemp and offer it for sale was the Humboldt Brewing Company from California, run by siblings David and Andy Ardell. When I interviewed them for this book, the Ardell brothers told me that they used toasted hemp seeds to give the base brown ale style a "unique, herb-accented flavor." Humboldt launched the beer in the mid- to late-1990s and called it, appropriately, Hemp Ale (fig. 4.1). It did not contain CBD or other cannabinoids, nor did it have the aroma of hemp, but Hemp Ale had a unique flavor and plenty of talk value at the time it was launched and for several years afterward. Humboldt's Hemp Ale continues to be brewed with toasted hemp seeds and enjoyed by fans, even after legalization of recreational cannabis in its home state of California.

The next big leap in the use of hemp in alcoholic craft beer occurred in 2015, when a Colorado cannabis enthusiast named Mason Hembree wanted to create a platform for serving CBD.

Figure 4.1. The original labeling for the Hemp Ale brand, brewed by Humboldt Brewing Company. *Courtesy of David and Andy Ardell.*

I was able to interview Hembree to get his story of how his hemp beer came to be. Hembree believed CBD had true medical value in reducing perceived pain and inflammation, and further believed that CBD would be the perfect agent to counter the inflammation caused by alcohol. Besides his own belief in the power of CBD, Hembree relied on consumers' preexisting beliefs or experience, and knew it would be unwise to make explicit health claims about ethanol combined with CBD in his beers. He decided to open a brewpub to bring his theories to life, opening Dad and Dude's Breweria in Aurora, Colorado in 2015 and so launching the first beer brewed with hemp in the modern American era. Hembree and his brewer, Brian Connelly, created many recipes that incorporated hemp into their three-barrel brewing system. They made sure to send their finished beers to a certified lab to verify that THC was not detectable, and to quantify the amount of CBD. According to Hembree when I interviewed him, the lab analysis revealed that each 12-ounce bottle of beer contained 4.2 mg of CBD.

Hembree carried out numerous trials, and the final, successful process was unique enough that he decided to file a patent in 2015 to protect his intellectual property. Although an invention is not fully protected until a patent is granted, Hembree could have started brewing and packaging with labels that stated "patent pending." However, Hembree decided to wait for full, legal protection and so he had to re-file in 2017 to keep the provisional "patent pending" status alive. The patent application is currently pending until the United States Patent and Trademark Office decides to review it and make a ruling. The specifics of how Hembree brews with hemp to extract and obtain a consistent CBD content in the beer will remain a mystery until the final patent is granted.

Of all the hemp beer recipes that Dad and Dude's Breweria created, the only one that was officially offered for sale was an IPA named George Washington's Secret Stash (fig. 4.2). This IPA was appropriately named, since the first American president's Mt. Vernon property not only had a small brewery, it was also a site where hemp was grown. Some stories allege that Washington incorporated hemp into some of his brewing recipes. George Washington's Secret Stash was offered at the 2016 Great American Beer Festival® and resulted in long lines of curious beer drinkers eager to taste the new cannabis brew. It was never entered into a judging category and so never stood to win a medal.

The story of George Washington's Secret Stash goes a little deeper. According to Hembree, he decided to file the appropriate paperwork for recipe and label approval from the federal Alcohol and Tobacco Tax and Trade Bureau (TTB), which, surprisingly, approved his request. However, after

Figure 4.2. Dad and Dude's hemp beer, General Washington's Secret Stash.
Courtesy of Mason Hembree.

internal discussions, the TTB reversed its decision and asked Hembree to formally withdraw his request, surrender his approval, and discontinue brewing his CBD IPA. After consulting with his attorney, Hembree refused to surrender his recipe. Figuring he was in a legal gray area, Hembree disregarded numerous threats from the TTB to revoke the recipe as he believed he had the legal right to brew the approved recipe.

After a few years of hard work to ensure the beer met all the appropriate guidelines and, most importantly, contained no THC, Hembree officially put the beer on tap and for sale at Dad and Dude's Breweria in 2018. People loved it. Plans were made to expand production and distribution throughout the United States, and beer distributors were excited to carry it. However, the legal issues kept mounting and Hembree soon halted expansion plans.

Over the next few months, news and announcements from Dad and Dude's stopped and things became very quiet. In March of 2019, the brewpub and recipe were reported to have been sold to a cannabis company from California,[*] but that did not come to fruition. Later that year, the brewpub property and equipment were seized by the city of Aurora, Colorado. Hembree told me he maintains ownership of his intellectual property and is counting the days until he receives a patent for his process to brew cannabis beer.

[*] Jonathan Shikes, "Dad & Dude's Breweria Closes; Future of Its CBD Beer Uncertain," *Westword,* October 22, 2019, 8:54 a.m., https://www.westword.com/restaurants/dad-and-dudes-breweria -closes-future-of-its-cbd-beer-uncertain-11518546.

USING CBD IN BEVERAGES

Much like liquid hop extract, CBD and other cannabinoids have an oily, sticky texture when extracted from the cannabis plant, and these oils do not readily mix with water and water-based beverages. Therefore, any brewer who uses cannabinoids or cannabis extracts in the brewing process must figure out a way to get the oily components into beer successfully. Certainly, innovators like Mason Hembree proved that processes exist or can be created (see "Hemp Ale and Washington's Secret Stash" sidebar), but some of the known processes are not suitable for the food industry. Additionally, most processes to make cannabis oil mixable with aqueous liquids are proprietary, such as one for water soluble cannabinoids (Martin, Razdan, and Mahadevan 2008), or classified as trade secrets.

In layman's terms, emulsification is simply the forced mixing of two liquids that normally do not mix together, such as oil and water. For example, when a chef is making a vinaigrette dressing it is necessary to add an emulsifier so that the oil fraction does not separate from the vinegar (water-based) fraction. In this case, many chefs will use a small amount of egg yolk or honey, or more refined ingredients such as xanthan gum or soy lecithin, to emulsify or "mix" the two immiscible ingredients. The end result is a salad dressing that is well blended and pours smoothly without separating because the oil has been formed into microscopic droplets that remain stable in suspension. The same can be done with cannabis oils. Although most cannabis emulsification processes are proprietary, they can generally be grouped into two categories: a conventional emulsification process, and a more complex process that makes CBD water compatible.

Emulsification of CBD

The first method to emulsify CBD is to mix the extract with a specific amount of emulsifying agent, such as vegetable gum. This is mixed at a very high speed, sometimes using ultrasonic waves, to create a stable solution that can be mixed into aqueous solutions like beer. While the final CBD oil solution can remain stable for weeks or months, eventually it will settle out in the same way many oil-vinegar dressings do when they have been sitting on grocery store shelves for a long time. Settling out or "layering" of the oil and water components causes inhomogeneity that can only be reversed by agitation, clearly undesirable for a beer or soda. To ensure that every serving contains a reasonably consistent amount of bioactive "oily" molecules, it is imperative to verify that the CBD oil solution does not settle out during the time between mixing and packaging. This forced mixing is similar to the naturally occurring "ouzo effect" (see sidebar). Depending on the emulsifier, the final product can be milky white or have a slightly hazy appearance due to the presence of very small, microemulsified oil droplets.

The Ouzo Effect

The ouzo effect is a natural example of spontaneous emulsification that occurs when water is added to a liqueur that contains highly hydrophobic essential oils, such as ouzo or limoncello, and the mixture changes from a clear liquid to a slightly milky looking solution. In theory, the hydrophobic oils should slowly join together in a process called coalescing until complete separation takes place, revealing an oil phase and a water phase. However, it is possible in some cases to create a stable colloid where oils form very small droplets that stay in suspension rather than joining together.

The scientific explanation of this observation is that the clear liqueur begins as a stable solution of hydrophobic essential oils in ethanol. However, when a small amount of water is added, it pulls some of the water-soluble ethanol away from the oil phase, causing the oils to form hydrophobic microscopic droplets that remain in stable solution but result in the solution taking on a milky white appearance. Scientists have determined that the size of the microscopic oil droplets can range from about 1 to 10 microns (Vitale and Katz 2003, 4108).

Note that the use of ethanol as the carrier might present a challenge from regulators, but TTB has recognized a blanket exemption for small amounts of ethanol used to make hop extracts soluble in beer. So, this could change in the future.

Water-Compatible CBD

The second method for emulsification is to make the cannabis oil into a more water-compatible mixture. This is not the same as water soluble. For example, a compound that is water soluble, like table salt (sodium chloride, chemical formula NaCl) will dissolve in water by dissociating into separate ions of sodium (Na^+) and chloride (Cl^-) and not affect the clear appearance of the water. An oily compound, such as cannabis extract, will never dissolve in water, but can appear to dissolve under the right conditions. This is called water compatibility.

Water compatibility also involves emulsification, but it requires more complex ingredients and methodologies. The aim is to form nanoparticles, that is, particles much smaller than the microparticles seen in conventional emulsification. In speaking with anonymous sources in the cannabis emulsification industry, I found that the main strategy for this concept emerged from the former Soviet Union, with the technology becoming more widely available after the country's breakup in 1991. In short, Soviet scientists discovered that a specific form of vitamin E known as d-α-tocopherol could be combined with other ingredients and then subjected to ultrasonic mixing to form nanoparticles, called micelles, that contained vitamin E. Micelles are extremely small, globular objects that have a lipophilic ("oil-loving") core and hydrophilic ("water-loving") outer shell; they are very stable and water compatible. Vitamin E is an oily compound that does not readily dissolve in water. The critical aspect of the Soviet scientists' discovery was that the micelles could be made to contain small amounts of oil-soluble compounds, such as certain drugs, providing a mechanism that allowed these compounds to readily pass through the cell membrane structures of the human body and deliver them to desired targets with a high degree of speed and efficiency.

According to two cannabis processors I spoke to, one application of this method involved doping athletes with steroids using this highly effective delivery system, and the athletes displayed the effects within minutes. These athletes could theoretically get tested for steroids prior to an event, then drink a liquid that looked like water that had nanoparticles of steroids for quick uptake immediately prior to a competition. This method was difficult to recognize because most performance steroids at the time had to be delivered by injection. More recently, researchers have found that this technology is suitable for the delivery of anticancer drugs and other helpful pharmaceuticals into the human body, especially since the FDA has approved its use as a safe pharmacological adjuvant (Guo et al. 2013).

In the world of cannabis, it is easy to see that the micelle emulsification technology can be used to create nanoparticles of cannabinoids that are water compatible, and therefore able to be put into beverages. Indeed, it appears that some suppliers are using these methods, creating products that have an almost crystal-clear appearance yet contain relatively high doses of CBD. I have tested at least one such product and found it to be very compatible with beer and it does not cause problems with haze or foam over its six-month shelf life, even though the oily characteristics of CBD would predict poor foam stability.

In addition to appearance and accurate and consistent dosing, the important aspect of the emulsification process is that the nanoparticles increase the bioavailability of pharmaceuticals, which could include cannabinoids, by delivering them into the body more efficiently (Guo et al. 2013). This is unlike cannabinoids ingested through edibles, which can take up to two hours to get into the bloodstream because they go through the digestive tract and can be altered into a more potent form by the liver (Huestis 2007).

The flavor of the final product can also be affected greatly by the type of CBD that is used in the emulsion. If the CBD is a pure distillate then flavor-active terpenes are not captured and the resulting product usually has no or very low aroma, but a slightly bitter taste due to the natural bitterness of cannabinoids. This natural bitterness does not usually lead to a palatable flavor in sweet beverages, but can complement drinks that are inherently bitter, such as beer, coffee, and tea. CBD might also be isolated as a full-spectrum or a broad-spectrum (or crude) extract rather than a distillate. A full-spectrum extract refers to a complete extract of the plant and will therefore also contain whatever THC was present, which should be below the legal limit of 0.3% THC by dry weight. A broad-spectrum CBD extract refers to an extract from the plant that has all cannabinoids except THC and is usually extracted from industrial hemp that contains less than 0.3% THC. Either extract will generally have a bitter taste because of the naturally bitter tasting cannabinoids. Both extracts can be refined to remove any aromatic terpenes and, thus, can either smell like cannabis or have no aroma.

Wine is not considered a bitter beverage, but at least one winery has been busy creating CBD-infused versions of its wines. This raises the question of how to balance the flavors so that the wine is not overtly bitter. The answer can possibly be found in the form of "bitterness blockers." These blocking agents are found naturally in certain plants, such as mushrooms, and work by either masking bitter flavors, altering the perception of bitterness, or preventing bitter compounds from interacting and binding to taste buds on the tongue that detect this flavor. It is also conceivable that the tannins in wine help minimize the bitter effect of cannabinoids. In general, bitterness blockers can work very well to allow the use of cannabinoids in beverages and foods. However, there are some beverages, such as soda and flavored waters, where it can be very difficult to employ this strategy because of the simpler flavor profiles of these beverages. In these cases, other emulsifiers must be tested, such as alternative vegetable gums or other oils. In addition, other bitterness blockers should be explored, which can include alternative sweeteners or even salt or salt substitutes.

Bitterness Blockers

Cannabinoids are bitter tasting, which can be problematic when they are emulsified into lighter and non-bitter beverages, such as flavored water, because they lead to a bitter off-taste in the final product. There are a few ways to solve this problem including masking, altering the perception of bitterness, or preventing bitter compounds from binding to taste buds on the tongue. Masking involves the use of traditional flavorings like salt or sugar, or the use of synthetic flavors such as GIV3616,[*] to mask the bitter flavor. Altering the perception of bitterness involves using adenosine monophosphate, which blocks the gustducin protein that normally functions in the mouth to register bitter-tasting compounds.[†] Prevention of bitter taste involves the use of mushroom extracts to temporarily bind to bitter taste receptors on the tongue, which prevents bitter compounds from being detected in the mouth.

[*] Stephanie Pappas, "New Bitterness Blocker Makes Food Seem Sweeter," Live Science, March 29, 2011, https://www.livescience.com/13450-bitter-blockers-processed-foods.html.

[†] "Bitter blocker backed by FDA," FoodNavigator, September 20, 2004, last updated March 14, 2017, https://www.foodnavigator.com/Article/2004/09/20/Bitter-blocker-backed-by-FDA.

WHY INCLUDE CBD IN BEER?

Aside from creating a naturally bitter-tasting beverage like beer that can lead to intoxication, there are several reasons that a brewer might choose to include CBD. In the case of Dad and Dude's Breweria, Mason Hembree wanted to use the perceived curative power of cannabis to reduce inflammation and provide pain relief to customers. Hembree did not make any health claims for his beer. Studies exist showing that CBD and other cannabinoids can provide relief from inflammation and pain (see further reading at the end of this chapter). Additionally, the perceived relaxing effect of CBD is something consumers look for; in the same way someone enjoys an alcoholic drink after work, someone can enjoy a non-alcoholic CBD beer while winding down from a stressful day at the office. Another reason to include CBD in beers is to provide a more flavorful experience when combining it with flavor-active hemp terpenes, so that the final product has an aroma of cannabis to complement the effect of CBD and the flavors of the beer. Certain terpenes, while non-intoxicating, have been suggested to work in conjunction with cannabinoids to amplify physiological effects (Russo 2011). Finally, CBD in a non-alcoholic beer has an allure due to its novelty, and customers may appreciate the convenience of a ready-to-drink beverage with CBD.

One argument in favor of using CBD is the suggestion that cannabinoids help cancer patients relieve the nausea caused by oncology treatments. Cannabinoids do this by inhibiting stimulation of neurones affected by signals from the vagus nerve, thereby greatly diminishing the need to vomit, or the "dry heaves" (Sharkey et al. 2014, 138–139). Although cannabinoids can be a source of extreme relief for oncology patients, this same effect can be detrimental during a binge drinking episode, when the body would normally react to excessive alcohol intake by forcefully expelling the contents of the stomach. In this scenario, the absence of vomiting could lead to alcohol poisoning, a very dangerous outcome. For this reason, **extreme caution should be taken before combining cannabis with alcohol**.

LABELING AND PACKAGING

Labeling Challenges

Some companies that offer cannabis beverages usually state very clearly that CBD is a major part of the ingredients. After the passage of the 2018 farm bill, many producers were careful to label any CBD as hemp-derived CBD or, rather, as hemp extract. Additionally, FDA guidelines stated that CBD cannot be legally introduced into food and beverages destined for human consumption. However, after the farm bill passed, the FDA's practice appeared to focus its limited enforcement resources on CBD beverages for which specific health claims were being made. This was interpreted as "permission" for CBD products to be offered for sale in the US as long as health claims were avoided. Currently, CBD products available for consumption can be purchased in numerous retail outlets and online. However, it is not without risk for the sellers as there have been several instances where FDA authorities presented cease and desist orders to retailers in multiple states.[1] The

---

[1] "FDA Warns 15 Companies Illegally Selling Various Products Containing Cannabidiol As Agency Details Safety Concerns," Press Announcements, US Food And Drug Administration, November 25, 2019, https://www.fda.gov/news-events/press-announcements/fda-warns-15-companies-illegally-selling-various-products-containing-cannabidiol-agency-details.

FDA is very clear that health claims are not permitted and that it will take enforcement action against companies that make such claims. Anecdotal evidence and budtender experience are not science-based, and how cannabinoids interact in the human body is not well understood. Sadly, there are still companies that will take advantage of consumers desperately looking for a cure or treatment for their condition. A recent study by researchers in the UK found that of the over-the-counter (OTC) CBD products consumers were able to buy only 31% contained the amount of CBD that was stated on the label (Chesney et al. 2020). One can only wonder if the popularity of CBD is mainly due to advertising or the placebo effect. A different study conducted in the US found that 43% of the CBD products analysed were under what the label stated, with some containing negligible amounts; and about 26% contained more than the label claimed (Bonn-Miller et al. 2017). The researchers identified two other major issues. First, about one in five CBD products contained THC at measurable levels above the legal limit. Secondly, the amount of CBD contained in the OTC products was much lower than levels found to produce physiological effects in published studies. Generally, the OTC products contained 10–20 mg per serving, while previous clinical studies have found the minimum level of CBD necessary to give observable effects was 300 mg. As Chesney et al. (2020, 7) noted, 100 mg and 150 mg doses were found to be ineffective in pre-clinical trials involving anxiety relief. The key takeaway is that dosage is critical and consumers should take care to educate themselves.

Packaging Challenges

It is very important to ensure that the dosage in a CBD beverage is meaningful and that the potency is consistent. If potency tests over the course of the product's shelf life show a decrease in cannabinoid content, it is imperative that the cause be identified. In general, cannabinoid emulsion suppliers and packagers indicate that decreasing potency is due to either breakdown of the cannabinoid, settling out/stratification, or adhesion of the cannabinoid to the spray-on liner of the can that the beverage is packaged in. The breakdown of THC into non-psychoactive cannabinol has been studied in controlled storage samples of cannabis and the results show that the level of THC decreases 16.6% after one year of storage at room temperature and then a 26.8% decrease from the original level after two years of storage.[2] In the case of beverages packaged with a high amount of oxygen or stored at a high temperature, these conditions may lead to degradation in

---

[2] S.A. Ross and M.A. Elsohly, "CBN and D^9-THC concentration ratio as an indicator of the age of stored marijuana samples," United Nations Office on Drugs and Crime, December 1, 1999, https://www.unodc.org/unodc/en/data-and-analysis/bulletin/bulletin_1997-01-01_1_page008.html.

packaged products, but this route would be relatively slow. Although settling and stratification could be factors, the most likely cause for decreased potency is the adhesion of cannabinoids to the can liner. This issue is being studied by major can producers. Initial solutions are to use beverage cans with liners that minimize cannabinoid adhesion and use emulsions that have been tested to prevent or minimize cannabinoids from sticking to can liners. Obviously, another solution is to package cannabis beverages in glass bottles, where regulations allow.

Can Liners for Cannabinoid Emulsions

One emulsion supplier, Vertosa, has studied the cannabinoid adhesion issue in canned products. It found that, under pressure, hydrophobic polymer can liners will attract emulsion droplets that contain hydrophobic oil in their core.[*] Over time, this results in the loss of potency of canned beverages with cannabinoids. With these findings, Vertosa was able to create unique cannabis emulsions that do not adhere to various can liners.

[*] "Vertosa emulsions reduce potency loss in aluminum cans," Vertosa, February 6, 2020, https://vertosa.com/blog/reduce-cannabinoid-potency-loss-in-cans.

FURTHER READING

D.C. Hammell, L.P. Zhang, F. Ma, S.M. Abshire, S.L. McIlwrath, A.L. Stinchcomb, and K.N. Westlund, "Transdermal cannabidiol reduces inflammation and pain-related behaviours in a rat model of arthritis," *European Journal of Pain* 20, no. 6 (July 2016): 936–948, https://doi.org/10.1002/ejp.818.

E.B. Russo, "Cannabinoids in the management of difficult to treat pain," *Therapeutics and Clinical Risk Management* 4, no. 1 (February 2008): 245–259, https://doi.org/10.2147/tcrm.s1928.

Sonja Vučković, Dragana Srebro, Katarina Savić Vujović, Čedomir Vučetić, and Milica Prostran, "Cannabinoids and pain: new insights from old molecules," *Frontiers in Pharmacology* 9 (November 2018): 1259, https://doi.org/10.3389/fphar.2018.01259.

Wei Xiong, Tanxing Cui, Kejun Cheng, Fei Yang, Shao-Rui Chen, Dan Willenbring, Yun Guan, et al., "Cannabinoids suppress inflammatory and neuropathic pain by targeting α3 glycine receptors," *Journal of Experimental Medicine* 209, no. 6 (May 2012): 1121–1134, https://doi.org/10.1084/jem.20120242.

5

CANNABINOID AND TERPENOID EFFECTS

Historically, humans have consumed many different substances for relaxation or intoxication. Alcohol is an example of an inebriant that has been used since at least 7,000 BCE and consumed in the form of fermented beverages (McGovern 2003, 314). The discovery of the "active," flammable ingredient, ethanol, occurred in the Middle East during the ninth century, when distillation was used to purify alcohol for use in medicine (al-Hassan 2001, 65–69). Other plants, such as the nightshade family of plants or opium poppies, have long been known to provide mind altering experiences when consumed in various forms, and their respective active ingredients, the hallucinogenic alkaloid hyoscyamine and the psychoactive alkaloids of opiates, were identified in the 1800s and used for medicinal purposes (Kohnen-Johannsen 2019, sec. 2.1). However, in the matter of the cannabis plant, people understood that the smoke from cannabis affected the mind and body, but the active ingredients that caused this effect were not isolated until at least the 1940s. Interestingly, it was not until the 1980s that researchers began to understand how and why it worked inside the human body.

CANNABINOIDS

Over the long period of time that cannabis has remained illegal under federal law in the US, the chemical structures of the two most studied cannabinoids, delta-9-tetrahydrocannabinol (THC) and cannabidiol (CBD), were finally made clear in the 1960s by researchers in Israel. The structure of CBD was studied and figured out in 1963 (Mechoulam and Shvo 1963), while THC was isolated and its structure elucidated the following year at the same research institute (Gaoni and Mechoulam 1964). These two compounds, known for causing intoxication (THC) and pain relief (CBD), form the basis for the majority of business in recreational and medical marijuana markets around the world where cannabis has been legalized. The scientific unraveling of the cannabis plant's physiological effects started in 1988 when researchers identified specialized cell receptors in the brain that bind to molecules from cannabis, called cannabinoids, and so cause physiological changes (Devane et al. 1988). Although these first studies were carried out with rats, it was hypothesized that the same cannabinoid receptors were active in the human brain. This early research led to the theory that THC from cannabis acted on the body by binding to cannabinoid receptors in the brain to cause euphoria and intoxication.

To scientists, the mechanism of marijuana cannabinoid effects on humans became clearer thanks to the discovery of cannabinoid receptors. But the bigger question was, why do human beings have cannabinoid receptors in their brains at all? In other words, it appeared as if humans, and other mammals, were hardwired to react to cannabinoids but for reasons unknown. Within a few short years, researchers found the answer. It turned out that the human body produces endogenous endocannabinoids, so called because they originate inside of the body, that bind to the cannabinoid receptors. The first such endocannabinoid was identified in 1992 and named anandamide, after the Sanskrit word $\bar{a}nanda$, which translates to "joy" and "bliss" (Devane et al. 1992, n.11). Other cannabinoids produced by the human body were soon identified.

When a second receptor for cannabinoids was discovered by researchers, it was named cannabinoid receptor 2, or CB_2, with the first receptor discovered being CB_1. The original CB_1 receptors function as part of the central nervous system, while both CB_1 and CB_2 receptors exist in the periphery of the body outside of the central nervous system (Pertwee 1997, 130). Over time, researchers referred to the complicated internal system involving endocannabinoids and cannabinoid receptors as the endocannabinoid system (ECS).

In humans, the ECS regulates physiological processes within the body, including pain, mood, and appetite (Pacher, Bátkai, and Kunos 2006). The ECS is activated by different mechanisms of action, which lead to corresponding reactions in the body. For example, it is believed that yoga works because the stretching and relaxing techniques activate the ECS and lead to a reduction in stress and a feeling of bliss, perhaps from the production of endocannabinoids.[1]

Some endocannabinoids lead to better moods and happiness. Another molecule of a type similar to endocannabinoids is palmitoylethanolamide (PEA), which has been researched in regard to pain management in humans (Hesselink 2012). PEA affinity for the CB_1 or CB_2 receptors is not very strong and so it is not considered a classic endocannabinoid. However, PEA appears to modulate ECS function, working in conjunction with anandamide in a type of "entourage effect" to reduce inflammation and pain (Bouaziz et al. 2017, 77).

Promising research has been conducted showing that some phytocannabinoids (i.e., cannabinoids derived from plants) when used at higher doses can be effective at alleviating complications from several diseases. It should be noted that the World Health Organization released a statement indicating that "CBD is generally well tolerated with a good safety profile" (WHO 2017, 5). Others have reported that sustained, high dosages of CBD, up to 1500 mg per day, are safe and well tolerated (Bergamaschi et al. 2011).

One example of the potential of phytocannabinoids comes from scientists at the Salk Institute, who found that THC from marijuana can facilitate the removal of amyloid beta from brain cells (Currais et al. 2016). Amyloid beta is the plaque-forming protein associated with Alzheimer's and thought to be the cause of the various debilitating aspects of the disease. Needless to say, the removal of this toxic protein could bring relief to millions of elderly people and their families around the world. Another area of promise is inflammatory diseases, which include ailments such as asthma, celiac disease, and hepatitis. Studies have found that CBD minimizes inflammation in the body and provides relief with inflammatory diseases (Burstein 2015). Additionally, research in mice suggests the anti-inflammatory properties of CBD may help to ward off the effects of the "cytokine storm" associated with COVID-19, which

---

[1] Liz Scherer, "Feeling Blissed Out After a Yoga Session? The Reason May Lie Within the Body's Endocannabinoid System," Everyday Health, January 30, 2020, https://www.everydayhealth.com/marijuana/feeling-blissed-out-after-a-yoga-session-the-reason-may-lie-within-the-bodys-endocannabinoid-system/.

causes excessive lung inflammation and destruction of lung tissue, a condition known as acute respiratory distress syndrome (ARDS). The researchers found mice injected with CBD had their ARDS symptoms partially or totally reversed (Salles et al. 2020). Since ARDS is one of the main causes of serious complications and death in cases of COVID-19 and other respiratory diseases, any treatment that eliminates the need for ventilators and helps lungs to recover from inflammatory-induced damage would be welcome.

A final note on inflammation involves diabetes. Diabetes is a quickly expanding disease in the developed world and, if not treated, can lead to amputation of limbs and/or death. Research has shown that several phytocannabinoids have the potential to relieve the inflammation that leads to the development of diabetic complications, including neuropathic pain (Horváth et al. 2012).

In fact, there are many phytocannabinoids that may have promising health benefits: cannabidiol (CBD); cannabichromene (CBC); cannabigerol (CBG); cannabinol (CBN), which is the breakdown product of THC; cannabidivarin (CBDV); and delta-9-tetrahydrocannabivarin (THCV). Research is being conducted by public and private laboratories to try to link specific phytocannabinoids with physiological processes in the human body (table 5.1). However, as there are more than 100 different cannabinoids that have been identified in the cannabis plant (Lafaye et al., 2017), much more work needs to be done to identify the pharmacological effects of these compounds.

Table 5.1 Selected cannabinoids and their main pharmacological

Cannabinoid	Effect
THC (Δ-9-tetrahydrocannabinol)	Psychoactive agent, analgesic, antinausea agent, anti-inflammatory
CBD (cannabidiol)	Antipsychotic, analgesic, antinausea agent, antibiotic, antispasmodic, anxiolytic, anticancer agent
CBC (cannabichromene)	Anti-inflammatory, antibiotic, antifungal, analgesic
CBG (cannabigerol)	Antifungal, antibiotic, anti-inflammatory, analgesic
CBN (cannabinol)	Anti-inflammatory, anticonvulsant, sedative
CBDV (cannabidivarin)	Anticonvulsant
THCV (Δ-9-tetrahydrocannabivarin)	Analgesic, psychoactive agent
Source: Brenneisen (2007).	

While cannabinoids were first isolated and identified in cannabis, other plants have also been found to produce cannabinoids and cannabinoid-like compounds, many of which have been used in folk medicines. For example, several *Rhododendron* species produce bioactive cannabinoids with sesquiterpene moieties, and have been used in traditional medicines in China and Mongolia for treatment of bronchitis and for producing stimulating tonics. Licorice root (*Glycyrrhiza*), liverworts, and flowering plants of the family Asteraceae (the daisy family) are other examples of plants that produce bioactive compounds with cannabinoid backbones (Gülck and Møller 2020, 987). Caution should be used with any of these types of plants that contain bioactive compounds because, for any potential benefit that may result from their use, there is the possibility of overdosing, sickness, and/or death.

TERPENES AND TERPENOIDS

Whether the aroma of cannabis is described as grassy, herbal, or dank, all of these smells emanate from terpenes, terpenoids, esters, and thiols. The aroma of hops can be citrussy, herbal, or tropical—again, these all emanate from the same general suite of compounds. Terpenes and terpenoids are compounds produced predominantly in nature by plants, including cannabis. It is thought that terpenes and terpenoids are an evolutionary development that provide plants with a defense mechanism against natural predators, a reproductive mechanism to attract insects for pollination, and even to attract larger predators to devour pests doing damage to the plant.

Technically, terpenes are hydrocarbons (i.e., consisting only of carbon and hydrogen), whereas terpenoids are terpenes with additional functional groups that include oxygen. The two terms are often used interchangeably. Terpenoids are numerous in nature, especially in the plant kingdom, and are the largest group of chemicals that have been isolated from plants, with up to 20,000 identified (Langenheim 1994, 1224).

Plants biosynthesize terpenoids using two metabolic pathways: the mevalonate route and the MEP/DOXP route. Both pathways result in two precursor compounds that are critical for terpenoid synthesis: isopentenyl pyrophosphate (IPP) and dimethylallyl pyrophosphate (DMAPP). Both IPP and DMAPP combine to create geranyl pyrophosphate, then this molecule is further elongated by combining it with more IPP. The result is a series of different length building blocks that are used to form terpenes and terpenoids in plants via the action of enzymes called terpene synthases (Pazouki and Niinemets 2016, 1–2).

Volatile terpenoids have long been believed to have pharmacological effects on humans. It was not until recently that researchers demonstrated that terpenoids, being lipophilic ("oil-loving"), can easily cross cell membranes and the blood-brain barrier, and that inhaled terpenes have a measurable effect on physiology in mammals (Andre, Hausman, and Guerriero 2016, 6; Buchbauer et al., 1991). For example, laboratory mice who inhaled the monoterpene alcohol linalool showed a significant decrease in activity, demonstrating linalool's effect as a type of relaxant (Buchbauer et al. 1991). Significant behavioral effects of terpenes on humans have also been demonstrated. In 1995, a citrus fragrance with high concentrations of the monoterpene limonene was administered to patients who had been diagnosed and hospitalized for depression. During the test, 9 out of 12 patients were successfully weaned off of medication for depression (Komori et al. 1995). It is important to note that limonene enters the bloodstream when inhaled, a fact demonstrated when significant amounts of limonene were detected in the bloodstream of human subjects exposed to limonene by inhalation (Falk-Filipsson et al. 1993). Finally, the monoterpene camphene has been shown to lower blood cholesterol and triglycerides in laboratory animals (Vallianou et al. 2011). It is expected that humans would react in a similar manner when exposed to camphene, which may replace or work in conjunction with current drugs used to treat high cholesterol (Vallianou et al. 2011, 2).

Table 5.2 shows several of the major terpenoids from cannabis and their various properties. It is interesting that myrcene, as one of the most common terpenes in both cannabis and hops, is believed to lead to sedation and sleep, with researchers having demonstrated that myrcene increases the onset of sleep in mice (Gurgel do Vale et al. 2002). In Belgium, "sleep pillows" can be purchased, which are small pillows filled with hops and designed to be placed under a regular bed pillow to help a person sleep (fig. 5.1). Cannabis and

Figure 5.1. Modern example of a sleep pillow filled with hops to aid in sleeping, purchased in the hop growing region of Poperinge, Belgium. The small size, as shown relative to two hop flowers, is typical. *Photograph by Jodi Villa.*

hop plant species are both in the family Cannabaceae and produce several of the same terpenes and terpenoids (Nuutinen 2018).

Table 5.2 Selected major terpenoids from *Cannabis* spp. and their physiological effects

Terpenoid	Effect
β-Myrcene	Anti-inflammatory, pain relief, sedative/sleep aid, anxiolytic
d-Limonene	Anti-cancer, anxiolytic, and immune stimulant
Linalool	Analgesic, anxiolytic, anti-inflammatory, anticonvulsant
β-Caryophyllene	Anti-inflammatory, gastric cytoprotector
α-Pinene	Memory aid
Source: Andre, Hausman, and Guerriero (2016).	

ENTOURAGE EFFECT

An interesting phenomenon occurs when cannabinoids and terpenoids act on the human body in unison. For example, antidepressant and anxiolytic effects from the combination of terpenoids combined with cannabinoids have been observed (Ferber et al. 2020). This phenomenon is referred to as the "entourage effect." In other words, the effect from using the whole plant product and its "entourage" components is "more efficacious" than the effect from a single, isolated component (Ben-Shabat et al. 1998, 30). Table 5.3 lists some of the interactions reported to occur with cannabinoids and terpenoids in cannabis.

Table 5.3 Entourage effects of terpenoids in the presence of *Cannabis* cannabinoids THC and CBD.

Terpenoid	Effect
β-Myrcene	Intoxication, sedating, muscle relaxant, anti-inflammatory
Linalool	Antianxiety, sedating, pain relief
Limonene	Antianxiety, immunostimulant, antibiotic
α-Pinene	Memory aid, bronchodilator, anti-inflammatory
β-Caryophyllene	Gastric cytoprotector, addiction aid, antimalarial
Humulene	Appetite suppressant, anti-inflammatory
Source: Russo (2011).	

The entourage effect is a major reason why many marijuana consumers are proponents of either full-spectrum marijuana (containing all cannabinoids from the plant) or broad-spectrum marijuana extracts (containing all cannabinoids except THC). Having the presence of many cannabinoids and terpenes is reported to amplify the effects of any positive physiological reactions and mitigate the effects of any negative cannabis experiences (Ben-Shabat et al. 1998, 30).

TOXICITY AND ADVERSE EFFECTS

Although some advocates for marijuana proclaim that no deaths have ever been recorded due to the use of marijuana, it is clear that this is incorrect. A notable example is driving while intoxicated from THC: persons testing positive for THC were three to seven times as likely to cause a motor-vehicle accident (fatal and non-fatal) as persons who had not used drugs or alcohol before driving (Volkow et al. 2014, 2222).

Cannabis has been linked to many negative outcomes and it would be irresponsible to only mention the positive. One study found an association between women who use cannabis while pregnant and their offspring who have a higher risk of autism spectrum disorder (Corsi et al. 2020). Children ten years of age who were exposed to cannabis *in utero* were found to be at higher risk of increased hyperactivity, inattention symptoms, and delinquency (Goldschmidt, Day, and Richardson et al. 2000). Cannabis use in adolescence has been linked to further negative outcomes, one being addiction, which itself leads to many other negative outcomes. It has been reported that heavy or long-term use of cannabis can lead to addiction in 17% of cases where people began using cannabis as adolescents. The same study reported that heavy and long-term users who started as adolescents also tended to have higher rates of unemployment and lower rates of satisfaction with their life (Volkow et al. 2014, 2221).

The effect of mixing alcohol and cannabis, typically referred to as "crossfading," can also have serious negative consequences. Research has shown that drinking alcohol prior to consuming cannabis leads to increased uptake of THC in the body and can intensify the high for the user (Hartman et al. 2015). The increased high can result in nausea and dizziness, which is why some users avoid crossfading, while other, more experienced users relish the experience when approached carefully. There is not much recent research showing the effects of using cannabis prior to drinking alcohol, but many users will admit that they do not feel as drunk when having alcohol while already high. This perception could lead to dangerous behaviors, including drunk driving. As already mentioned, (see p. 59), CBD is believed to minimize the gag reflex. Thus, combining marijuana and alcohol use can potentially lead to drinking excessive amounts of alcohol and alcohol poisoning.

Table 5.4 Negative effects of Short-term and
Long-term use of Cannabis

Effect of Short-Term Use
Impaired short-term memory – difficulty learning and retaining information
Impaired motor coordination – interference with driving skills and increasing risk of injuries
Altered judgement – increased risk of behaviors that facilitate the spread of STDs
Paranoia and anxiety – when using high doses

Effects of Long-Term or Heavy Use
Addiction
Altered brain development
Poor educational outcome
Impairment of cognition, particularly affecting short-term memory and executive functioning
Diminished life satisfaction and achievement
Increased risk of making outpatient visits for respiratory illness and injuries
Increased risk of chronic psychotic disorders
Lowers testosterone levels, impairs semen production, motility and viability

Sources: Volkow et al. (2014, 2220); Kalant (2004); ElSohly (2007).

As a final note of caution, cannabinoids, specifically THC, are active in the body for a relatively short amount of time but can remain detectable in the blood for a much longer period (Peng et al. 2020). Research has shown that frequent marijuana users can have at least 2 nanograms of THC per milliliter of blood in their system despite days of abstinence, which means the THC remains detectable for several days at levels above many jurisdictions' mandated legal minimums. Some users exhibit a "double hump" pattern, where there is an increase in detectable THC levels after several days of declining levels (Peng et al. 2020, 4). Since users experience a high that only lasts for several hours, the presence of THC in the blood after many days does not demonstrate that the user is still intoxicated. Researchers have reported that THC accumulates in fatty tissues in the body and that exercise and dieting do not release THC back into the blood or urine (Westin et al. 2014). Thus, a detectable level of THC will persist in the body for a while and there is no practical way for a marijuana user to quickly rid themselves of this.

The fact that THC can remain detectable in the blood many days after last using marijuana raises several legal questions. Primary among them is that the measured level of THC in the blood is not necessarily an accurate indicator for whether a person is intoxicated and unable to operate machinery or drive. The bottom line is that much more research has to be conducted in order to ensure that the general public is kept safe (accident prevention remains the goal for everyone), but also in order that marijuana users (including medical users) are not unfairly penalized by laws that focus solely on THC levels per se. With more states in the US legalizing cannabis, it is hoped that both private advocacy groups and governmental cannabis regulatory groups can provide the funding to carry out such research to inform future cannabis legislation.

It should be clear that the cannabis plant contains many compounds that are bioactive, that is, compounds that can cause physiological reactions either singularly or in unison with each other. It should also be clear that researchers are only just starting to understand how some cannabinoids and terpenoids cause pharmacological effects. The majority of these compounds in cannabis have not yet been studied in relation to their effects on the human body. Therefore, extreme caution should be taken by anyone wishing to use cannabis by itself or in combination with any drug, legal or illegal.

6

THE CURRENT LEGAL STATUS OF CANNABIS IN THE US

At the start of 2021 in the United States, marijuana remains illegal under federal law and falls under the jurisdiction of the US Drug Enforcement Administration (DEA). It is classified as a Schedule I drug under the Controlled Substances Act of 1970 and, as such, it is viewed as having no accepted medical use and a high potential for abuse and addiction. State penalties for marijuana offenses vary throughout the US, but the maximum federal penalties are severe and can include the death penalty for leaders of major marijuana operations. Some of these penalties are listed in table 6.1.

As we saw in chapter 1, the route that the federal government followed to make cannabis illegal appeared to be rooted in personal crusades, cronyism, and racism rather than thorough scientific analysis. Regardless of the justifications, until 2018 under federal law all forms of cannabis were illegal to possess or consume. In 2018, the Agriculture Improvement Act was signed into law and industrial hemp became legal as an agricultural product, as long as the THC content remained below the (arbitrarily assigned) 0.3% dry weight basis. The act also provided that hemp, as an agricultural commodity, would be under the jurisdiction of the FDA

Table 6.1 Maximum federal penalties regarding marijuana

Offense	Maximum Penalty	Maximum fine/imprisonment
Possession	Misdemeanor or Felony	US$5,000/3 years
Sale[a]	Felony	US$1,000,000/Life
Cultivation	Felony	US$1,000,000/Life
Paraphernalia	Felony	NA/3 years
Major criminal enterprise	Felony	US$4–10m/Life[b]/Death sentence[c]

Source: "Federal Laws and Penalties," NORML [National Organization for the Reform of Marijuana Laws], accessed November 30, 2020, https://norml.org/laws/federal-penalties-2/.

[a] Sales to a minor or within 1,000 feet of a school carry a double penalty.

[b] Max. fine and life imprisonment are for manufacture or distribution involving 1,000 cannabis plants or 1,000 kg or more.

[c] A sentence of death only applies to manufacture, importation, or distribution as part of a continuing criminal enterprise; AND the amounts must involve 66.14 US tons or more, or 60,000 cannabis plants, or gross receipts of US$20m in a 12-month period; AND the defendant must be a principal actor in the organization.

and USDA rather than the DEA.[1] Thus, hemp production needs to adhere to all standards and safeguards that apply to the food chain in the US, such as substances generally recognized as safe (GRAS) and processes that follow good manufacturing practices (GMPs). Note that this does not extend to hemp products not covered by the Agriculture Improvement Act of 2018. Thus, marijuana and cannabinoid-infused products produced for human consumption in states where it is legal to do so are subject to whatever safeguards that state has put in place to control for contaminants (e.g., pesticides, molds, and heavy metals), and these standards can vary widely from state to state (Seltenrich 2019).

CANNABIS IN MEDICINES, FOODS/BEVERAGES, AND SUPPLEMENTS

Homebrewers have experimented with the use of cannabis in homebrewed beers for many years. At first glance, a combination of alcohol and cannabis in the same product might seem a way to combine the best of both worlds. However, this combination is strictly prohibited in any commercially available products under both federal and state laws. The Alcohol and Tobacco Tax and Trade Bureau (TTB) does not allow the use of any substances in alcoholic beverages that are illegal under federal law, and the states that have legalized cannabis do not allow alcohol in any cannabis-containing beverages. Besides the obvious legal reasons, there are issues of risks to health—how do all of the

---

[1]   Agriculture Improvement Act of 2018, Pub. L. 115–334, title X, § 10113, 132 Stat. 4913 (2018).

cannabinoids in marijuana react in the body when alcohol is also present? The example of Four Loko (see pp. 17–18) demonstrates how some people can have serious medical problems when high levels of a psychotropic substance (i.e., caffeine) are combined with alcohol and ingested in a short time frame. In light of this, **anyone wishing to experiment with cannabis and alcohol in the same liquid should recognize the legal and health risks of doing so**.

A common misperception with the Agriculture Improvement Act is that any hemp-derived product is legal and can be used in food and beverages. However, it is important to know that under the Agriculture Improvement Act the only parts of the hemp plant that are currently allowed to be legally sold as food in the US are hemp seed products, which do not typically contain cannabinoids. These products include hulled hemp seeds, hemp seed protein powder, and hemp seed oil. The reason that all other parts of the hemp plant cannot be used in the food chain is that they contain cannabinoids, more specifically, CBD. As much as consumers want to buy and consume CBD products, the role of the FDA is to protect consumers from ingesting compounds that may be unsafe due to their physiological effects on the body, and to protect consumers from manufacturers who make unsubstantiated and misleading claims about their products, such as the ability to cure or treat diseases.

Coincidentally, certain preparations of CBD are currently classified as medicines because the FDA approved the drug Epidiolex in 2018. Epidiolex was tested successfully and is used to treat children over one year of age with rare and severe cases of seizures associated with Lennox-Gastaut syndrome, Dravet syndrome, and tuberous sclerosis complex (https://www.epidiolex.com/). Since CBD was not being previously used or sold as a dietary supplement in the US, it became classified solely as a drug by the FDA. If CBD had been previously used as a supplement per the 1994 Dietary Supplement Health and Education Act (DSHEA), then FDA approval as a dietary supplement would likely have been much easier and faster. Because it is classified as a medicine, the Federal Food, Drug, and Cosmetic Act (FDCA) makes it unlawful to put medicines into foods or dietary supplements that are sold interstate. Since the FDA currently considers CBD to be a drug, it requires clear and convincing evidence that CBD is safe to use as a dietary supplement prior to approving its use in the food chain.

Although putting CBD into foods or beverages is unlawful, the fact that the FDCA specifically limits interstate commerce provides a perceived loophole for any company willing to take a chance on selling CBD products within a single state. Clearly, there are foods and beverages infused with CBD being offered for sale in certain markets. However, some states have started to crack down on these activities by using their respective health departments to enforce food laws that are aligned with the FDCA. California and New York are among states who have started enforcing FDA rulings on CBD in the food chain.

The state of Colorado is one of the few states to have a policy allowing the use of the complete hemp plant, including CBD derived from industrial hemp, in the food chain under Colorado Revised Statute §35-61-108(2). This law does require that industrial hemp contain less than 0.3% THC by dry weight. Prior to the enactment of C.R.S. §35-61-108(2), any CBD products sold in dispensaries in Colorado were required to have a minimal amount of THC in order to be classified as marijuana, which, of course, ruled out the use of industrial hemp as a cannabis feedstock. It is too early to tell if Colorado's more permissive legislation is ahead of its time and will result in a slew of safe, marketable (food and drink) products that contain CBD, or result in some unforeseen negative medical reactions caused by CBD. The FDA realizes that many people are currently using CBD foods and drinks, so it is currently studying input from experts as to the safety of CBD as a supplement. In the near future, the FDA should have a definitive ruling on CBD and resulting guidance for its use in products for human consumption. Regardless of the outcome from the FDA, not everyone will be satisfied because of the highly controversial nature of cannabis. Some people will always believe in the healing properties of CBD, and others will be on the lookout for the next compound that shows promise for given ailments.

To summarize, products containing only CBD could not legally be sold in dispensaries in the state of Colorado prior to July 1, 2020. However, under C.R.S. §35-61-108(2), CBD-only products made from industrial hemp can now be sold in cannabis dispensaries in Colorado. Any other consumable products that do not contain THC-containing cannabis are still prohibited from being sold in Colorado dispensaries, including alcohol, water, and soda.

Working within Your State's Laws

CERIA Brewing Company (Arvada, Colorado) wanted to offer a non-alcoholic IPA with CBD prior to July 20, 2020 and found that it was prohibited to sell a CBD-only product in Colorado dispensaries. At that time, any CBD products were required to have a minimal amount of THC in order to be classified as marijuana. Since dispensaries offered a state-legal venue to sell cannabis products, and the general market was not a guaranteed venue without full FDA approval for CBD products, the decision was made to include THC in CERIA's IPA offering. In the end, a dosage of 10 mg CBD plus 10 mg THC was infused into every can and offered for sale in Colorado dispensaries. In accordance with state cannabis laws, no medical claims or health benefits were made on the label.

STATE REGULATIONS

In spite of the decades-long prohibition of marijuana, the majority of states in the US have passed laws that legalize the use of marijuana for medical and/or recreational purposes. A more detailed account of this history is given in chapter 1.

By April 2021, 36 US states and the District of Columbia operated legal medical marijuana markets, aimed at those who require marijuana for pain relief or relief from debilitating illnesses, such as cancer and epilepsy. By the same point in time, 16 states and the District of Columbia had approved recreational marijuana markets, allowing for the possession and consumption of marijuana by anyone over the age of 21.

Possession and Use of Marijuana

Figure 6.1 and table 6.2 illustrate the current state of legalization. This information is provided by DISA Global Solutions. As marijuana regulations seemingly change rapidly, DISA updates its site monthly to reflect new laws. Because of this, the site is a good source for those wanting to know what is and what is not legal (https://disa.com/map-of-marijuana-legality-by-state).

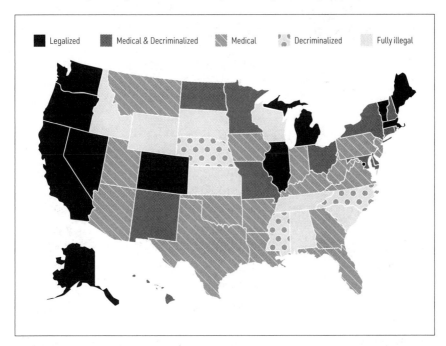

Figure 6.1. Map of the United States showing different types of cannabis legalization. *"Map of Marijuana Legality by State," DISA, accessed November 30, 2020, https://disa.com/map-of-marijuana-legality-by-state.*

Table 6.2 Legal status of marijuana in District of Columbia and the
50 states of the US

State	Legal Status	Medical	Decriminalized
Alabama	Fully Illegal	No	No
Alaska	Fully Legal	Yes	Yes
Arizona	Fully Legal	Yes	Yes
Arkansas	Mixed	Yes	No
California	Fully Legal	Yes	Yes
Colorado	Fully Legal	Yes	Yes
Connecticut	Mixed	Yes	Yes
Delaware	Mixed	Yes	Yes
District of Columbia	Fully Legal	Yes	Yes
Florida	Mixed	Yes	No
Georgia	Mixed	CBD Oil Only	No
Hawaii	Mixed	Yes	Yes
Idaho	Fully Illegal	No	No
Illinois	Fully Legal	Yes	Yes
Indiana	Mixed	CBD Oil Only	No
Iowa	Mixed	CBD Oil Only	No
Kansas	Fully Illegal	No	No
Kentucky	Mixed	CBD Oil Only	No
Louisiana	Mixed	Yes	No
Maine	Fully Legal	Yes	Yes
Maryland	Mixed	Yes	Yes
Massachusetts	Fully Legal	Yes	Yes
Michigan	Fully Legal	Yes	Yes
Minnesota	Mixed	Yes	Yes
Mississippi	Mixed	Yes	Yes
Missouri	Mixed	Yes	Yes
Montana	Fully Legal[a]	Yes	Yes[a]
Nebraska	Fully Illegal	No	Yes
Nevada	Fully Legal	Yes	Yes
New Hampshire	Mixed	Yes	Yes
New Jersey	Fully Legal	Yes	Yes
New Mexico	Mixed	Yes	Yes
New York	Fully Legal	Yes	Yes
North Carolina	Fully Illegal	No	Yes
North Dakota	Mixed	Yes	Yes

State	Legal Status	Medical	Decriminalized
Ohio	Mixed	Yes	Yes
Oklahoma	Mixed	Yes	No
Oregon	Fully Legal	Yes	Yes
Pennsylvania	Mixed	Yes	No
Rhode Island	Mixed	Yes	Yes
South Carolina	Fully Illegal	No	No
South Dakota	Fully Legal[a]	Yes[a]	Yes[a]
Tennessee	Fully Illegal	No	No
Texas	Mixed	CBD Oil Only	No
Utah	Mixed	Yes	No
Vermont	Fully Legal	Yes	Yes
Virginia	Mixed	CBD Oil Only	Yes
Washington	Fully Legal	Yes	Yes
West Virginia	Mixed	Yes	No
Wisconsin	Mixed	CBD Oil Only	No
Wyoming	Fully Illegal	No	No

Source: "Map of Marijuana Legality by State," DISA, accessed May 3, 2021, https://disa.com/map-of-marijuana-legality-by-state.

Notes: State status reflects current laws as of April 2021. "Decriminalized" status in states with fully legal cannabis status equates to "Recreational."

[a] Enactment is pending until future date.

It should be noted that the laws on cannabis in each state are sometimes not as simple as they appear in print. Anyone planning to consume marijuana should make sure they thoroughly understand their state laws beforehand. In fact, several states are becoming very strict when regulating both marijuana and hemp. For example, Iowa allows medical cannabis, and many people believe this permits them to enjoy any marijuana product and any type of hemp product. However, smokable hemp is prohibited in Iowa and possession of hemp flowers even carries a fine of US$1,825.[2] Presumably, this is because it is very difficult for police to distinguish hemp flowers from marijuana flowers, and the only form of cannabis that is legal is medical CBD oil. At least 12 other states have similar regulations banning smokable hemp.

-----

[2] "Smokable Hemp Leaves Lack of Clarity in the Hawkeye State," New Frontier Data, July 8, 2020, https://newfrontierdata.com/cannabis-insights/smokable-hemp-leaves-lack-of-clarity-in-the-hawkeye-state/.

Drug-Sniffing Dogs

When the topic of drug-sniffing dogs is discussed in regard to marijuana, the Fourth Amendment to the US Constitution is usually invoked. This amendment gives citizens and their possessions the right to protection from unreasonable search and seizure. With this in mind, it has been found that dogs can positively sniff out marijuana, whether it is in a person's pocket or in their automobile. Furthermore, for many years police used drug-sniffing dogs in airports or on active duty to help find marijuana. However, with the passage of the Agriculture Improvement Act of 2018, hemp can be in a person's possession legally. But federal law draws a distinction between hemp, which is legal, and marijuana, which is not: hemp has less than 0.3% dry weight THC, while marijuana has more than 0.3% dry weight THC. Aside from this arbitrary but legal difference, marijuana and hemp are the same plant with similar aromas. Because of this issue, drug-sniffing dogs cannot detect the difference between the two plants.* So, in practice, a person who might be in possession of legal hemp products could theoretically be stopped by a police officer and searched if a police dog detected cannabis. However, any lawyer would say that this amounts to unreasonable search and seizure and violates the Fourth Amendment. Courts agree and that is why drug-sniffing dogs are not seen as often as they were prior to 2018 (fig 6.2).

Figure 6.2. Drug-sniffing dogs are a vanishing breed in the US. *Dragos Cogocari/Getty Images.*

* Undercover Stoner, "Can Drug-Sniffing Dogs Tell the Difference Between Marijuana and Hemp?" Cannabis.net, September 17, 2020, https://cannabis.net/blog/opinion/can-drugsniffing-dogs-tell-the -difference-between-marijuana-and-hemp.

Growing Cannabis

The vagaries of state laws also extend to growing cannabis for marijuana. Anyone wanting to grow THC-containing marijuana should first check local laws to make sure that growing it is legal in their locale. If there is any doubt, then legal advice should be obtained. And remember, if the plant contains more than 0.3% THC by dry weight it remains a controlled substance under federal law regardless of the position of your state.

The growing of marijuana differs in those states where it is fully legal and generally involves practical rules to follow. For example, the state of Colorado allows each adult over the age of 21 to grow up to six plants for personal use, with no more than three plants flowering at one time.[3] A Colorado residence can have a maximum of 12 plants, regardless of the number of adults living at the same address. Additionally, growers in Colorado cannot grow outdoors and must keep the plants indoors and locked away from minors.

In contrast, the state of Oregon allows adults to grow no more than four marijuana plants in a single residence, regardless of the number of adults living at the residence.[4] Unlike Colorado's regulations, Oregon law does not appear to make a distinction between non-flowering and flowering plants. The penalty if caught growing more than four plants can be a fine of up to US$125,000 and time in prison. Stricter rules apply if you live within 1,000 feet of a school, as growing cannabis within this range is forbidden and, if caught, can result in up to US$375,000 in fines and up to 25 years in prison. From these two examples it is clear that growing cannabis involves thorough knowledge of the laws, even in states where recreational marijuana is legal.

It should also be stressed that marijuana laws appear to change more often than other regulatory laws. Whether this effect is real or perceived, a potential grower should at minimum perform an internet search of their state's most recent laws concerning the growing of cannabis, including different treatments for hemp and marijuana. This is important since some regulations may be present for hemp but not for marijuana, and vice versa. Growers can never be too careful regarding the law.

---

[3] "Home Grow Laws," Colorado Marijuana, Colorado Official State Web Portal, accessed November 30, 2020, https://www.colorado.gov/pacific/marijuana/home-grow-laws.

[4] Or. Rev. Stat. § 475B.301(1) (2019 Edition), https://www.oregonlegislature.gov/bills_laws/ors/ors475B.html.

STRANGE CANNABIS LAWS

Most of the regulations and laws surrounding cannabis can be confusing and sometimes intimidating. However, some regulations exist that leave a person wondering why the law was needed and if it was enacted due to some odd historical event.[5] For example, in California it is illegal to transport cannabis by aircraft or watercraft, as well as by drone or human-powered vehicle.[6] Obviously, any attempt at sustainability, such as delivery of cannabis by bicycle, is illegal. The cannabis can only be transported in an unmarked motor vehicle.

The state of Delaware makes it illegal to advertise medical cannabis pretty much anywhere, except in medical journals and phone books.[7] Bear in mind that phone book usage continues to dwindle due to the fact that phone book data is based on land lines, which are rapidly being replaced by cell phones, and people are using online searches instead.[8]

In Michigan, all legal documents pertaining to marijuana use the older spelling of "marihuana" with an *h*. Michigan's Marijuana Regulatory Agency (MRA), which ironically chooses to use the *j* spelling, bases this decision on the original spelling from the Marihuana Tax Act of 1937. Since the spelling was used in all legal documentation, the MRA indicates that it would take an act of the Michigan legislature to change the spelling.[9]

Washington, D.C. allows almost anyone to open a dispensary unless they sell or repair cars.[10] The limitation on auto mechanics and car dealers makes a person wonder why this group of people was isolated and identified as not worthy of opening and running a dispensary in the capital of the United States.

FINAL THOUGHTS

As a final note on the legalities of marijuana, many people question when full federal legalization will occur in the United States. At time of writing, many people believe that the Democratic Party is more open to approving legalization, while the Republican Party is not. By that logic, a government run with a

---

[5]   "The Oddest Cannabis Laws and Regulations," *Marijuana Politics*, 420 Intel, August 26, 2020, https://420intel.com/articles/2020/08/26/oddest-cannabis-laws-and-regulations.

[6]   Cal. Code Regs. tit. 16, § 5311(c) (2020), https://www.bcc.ca.gov/law_regs/bcc_notice_emerg.pdf.

[7]   Del. Code Ann. tit. 16, § 4919A(k) (2021).

[8]   Tamara Chuang, "Get your head out of the old phone book and figure out how to go online to find a person's phone number," *Denver Post*, January 29, 2018, 5:35 a.m., https://www.denverpost.com /2018/01/29/find-a-phone-number-2018/.

[9]   "Why is marijuana sometimes spelled with an 'h' and other times spelled with a 'j'?" Marijuana Regulatory Agency, accessed November 30, 2020, https://www.michigan.gov/mra/0,9306,7-386 -83746-449300--,00.html.

[10] D.C. Mun. Regs. tit. 22, § 5403.3.

Democratic Party majority will have a higher likelihood of ushering in federal approval, while a Republican-run government will tend to keep marijuana illegal. However, as explained in chapter 1 (p. 13), some people believe Internal Revenue Code Sec. 280E is a "cash cow" that brings in much-needed tax revenue. Because of this, and regardless of political affiliation, governmental officials may want to maintain marijuana's illegal status to keep money flowing to the government via Sec. 280E which imposes an effective tax rate of 70% on cannabis businesses.[11]

When Prohibition in the US was repealed in 1933, the federal government provided very stiff penalties for breaking the law. Any illegal distillers, so-called moonshiners, could face severe fines and many years in prison. This tough enforcement of the law allowed legal alcohol sales to flourish and led to the virtual elimination of illegal alcohol production. Perhaps a similar approach could work for marijuana legalization. Severe penalties for the illegal production and sale of cannabis could lead to the virtual elimination of the black market and allow the legal cannabis market to flourish. After all, money was the primary factor leading to the prohibition of cannabis in the twentieth century. Money will probably be the primary factor leading to the federal legalization of cannabis in the twenty-first century.

Finally, in states where both alcohol and cannabis are legal, one should question whether combining them in the same product is a safe thing to do. Perhaps in moderation it leads to a mellow, cross-fading session. In other situations, combining marijuana and alcohol can lead to serious or life-threatening outcomes (pp. 70–71). The bottom line is that experimentation in this new world of legal intoxicants must proceed with caution.

---

[11] Dennis Romero, "California's cannabis black market has eclipsed its legal one," NBC News, September 20, 2019, 4:01 a.m. CDT, https://www.nbcnews.com/news/us-news/california -s-cannabis-black-market-has-eclipsed-its-legal-one-n1053856; William Turvill, "'The legal stuff is garbage': why Canada's cannabis black market keeps thriving," Society, *Guardian*, March 18, 2020, 5:00 a.m. EDT, https://www.theguardian.com/society/2020/mar/18/cannabis-canada-legal -recreational-business.

7

REGULATORY COMPLIANCE

In the world of consumer-packaged goods, there are two major hurdles, among a long list of obstacles, to getting products into the hands of consumers. Both hurdles must be successfully overcome for a product to exist and be profitable in the marketplace. First, a supplier has to find the best way to get products onto the shelves of retailers—whether brick and mortar or virtual—so that consumers are able to make a purchase. Meetings and negotiations between salespeople and retailer representatives (called "buyers") can take several weeks or months before a product earns its spot on a retailer's shelf. This activity is often defined as the "sales" or "push" of business negotiations. Secondly, the supplier must create a desire within the customer to purchase their products by using clever advertising or through the packaging and messaging that takes place at the point of purchase. This effort is often defined as the "marketing" or "pull" of the product. Many sales and marketing tactics used in the American consumer-packaged goods market have created highly successful brands.

In highly regulated industries, such as alcoholic beverages, many restrictions exist for how a supplier can market and sell products. For example, the use of any statement, design, device, or representation that is "obscene or indecent" is prohibited,[1] although the government does not define what is indecent with regard to malt beverages. Additionally, if a beer is not fermented at a "comparatively high temperature" it cannot be labeled as an ale, porter, or stout in any advertisement, even though temperatures are not defined in the relevant section of the law.[2] It is assumed that the fermentation temperature of these ale products should be significantly higher than a lager-type product. For those in the know, this usually means fermentation temperatures of around 46–54°F (8–12°C) for lagers and 64–68°F (18–20°C) for ales. Further, any sampling of alcoholic beverages must follow state-specific laws. Some states do not allow sampling, while others limit sampling to only a few ounces.

Finally, at the point of purchase it is illegal for retailers to charge slotting fees for alcoholic beverages. Slotting fees are those additional charges a supplier pays to a retailer to ensure that the supplier's products are displayed on store shelves in a way that maximizes visibility and purchase rates. For example, optimum shelf height for children's cereal is among the lower shelves where it catches the attention of children who will pick up the package and ask their parents to purchase it. Optimum shelving for beer should be at adult eye level in the beer aisle or in an end-cap display at the end of an aisle, but it could also mean placing cases of beer near the meat department to encourage those planning to grill to pick up some extra beer. This type of synergistic product placement in grocery stores is known as cross-merchandising and is very effective at increasing sales for the retailer.

RECREATIONAL MARIJUANA LABELING REGULATIONS

If you thought labeling requirements for alcoholic beverages were complex, just wait. Requirements for cannabis-containing beverages will astound you. Products made with cannabis sold in the US are also tightly regulated, but at the state level since no regulations exist at the federal level due to cannabis still being illegal under federal law. Regulations for sales and marketing for products containing cannabis or cannabinoids can be difficult to interpret but must always be followed by companies wishing to be in good standing with state regulators. Many consumers who purchase products in a

---

[1] Prohibited practices, 27 C.F.R. § 7.29(a)(3) (2020).
[2] Class and type, 27 C.F.R. § 7.24(e) (2020).

dispensary are usually unaware of the rules that suppliers must follow in order to have their products among those offered for sale.

Required and Prohibited Language

If your experience is in the alcoholic beverages industry, labeling of cannabis beverages has some similarities to labeling of alcoholic beverages (depending on the state). Figure 7.1 shows the approved label for CERIA Grainwave, which is marketed as Belgian-style white ale for the Colorado market. This label serves as an illustrative example of the similarities and differences between labeling requirements for cannabis and alcoholic beverages.

Similarities include the following (an asterisk indicates mandatory information for a cannabis beverage label):

1. Company name
2. Brand name
3. Logo
4. Romance copy
5. Warning label*
6. Nutrition panel
7. Allergy statement*
8. Recycle statement

Differences include the following (an asterisk indicates mandatory information):

1. Potency label for active THC;* in figure 7.1 it shows 5 mg.
2. Universal THC warning symbol centered in the lower, front part of the label.*
3. A statement indicating it is a beverage, not a smokable product; here the statement reads "For oral consumption."
4. A statement indicating that the container is child-resistant and the opening instructions are on the can lid.
5. There is a blank panel on the lower left side of the label.* This is where an information panel is placed showing the milligram amounts of active THC and CBD in the product, as analyzed by a state-approved cannabis laboratory. Additionally, the batch number, license number, and production date, among other required information, must be listed.
6. A warning statement* wherein, among other required verbiage, it must state "The intoxicating effects of this product may be delayed by up to 4 hours."

Figure 7.1. Approved label for CERIA Grainwave Belgian-style white ale for the Colorado cannabis edibles market.

Overall, the labeling of cannabis beverages can seem a little strange in comparison to alcohol. For example, in Colorado a few of the labeling restrictions state that:[3]

- any text on a label must be in English;
- the words "candy" and "candies" are prohibited;
- THC content must be labeled in milligrams of active THC and CBD per serving. Measured potency must be within 15% of the target label potency.

With these examples in mind, one can see that cannabis labeling is regulated in a different manner than alcohol in the US. Hypothetically, if the cannabis requirement for English on a label were applied to the alcohol industry, an imported beer from Mexico would not be allowed to use the words "Cerveza Superior" as is used on the label of the most popular imported beer from south of the border, unless they provided the English translation of "Superior Beer." Additionally, following the same logic, an imported beer from Belgium, or a Belgian-style beer brewed by an American craft brewer, would not be allowed to say on the label that it is brewed with candi sugar because of the prohibition on the use of the word candy.

If following this same stringency for malt beverages, the TTB would allow a 15% variance up or down from the alcohol claim on the label. This is in stark contrast to the actual current alcohol variance allowed by the TTB of 0.3% up or down from the label claim (27 CFR § 19.356 (c)). However, unlike alcoholic drinks, which are regulated at the federal level, you must also allow for

---

3   1 Code Colo. Regs. § 212-3 R 3-1010 (2021).

differences in cannabis labeling laws from state to state. For example, while the allowable label variance for cannabis products in Colorado is no more than plus or minus 15% active THC, the state of California allows a variance of no more than plus or minus 10% active THC. These THC limits apply when the product is analyzed by state-certified cannabis test laboratories and can change depending on degradation of THC or whether or not the THC molecules adhere to the interior liner of the can, thus decreasing the amount of THC measured in the liquid fraction. Failure to have THC levels within the allowable limits leads to the product's label not being approved and it being unable to enter the market.

Furthermore, each state where recreational marijuana is legal has slightly different requirements for labeling marijuana beverages. For example, the state of Colorado is relatively lenient and allows marijuana beverage suppliers to put actual beer style descriptors on the label, along with beer terminology, and to declare that it is non-alcoholic. For instance, a non-alcoholic marijuana version of a stout can be labeled "non-alcoholic stout." However, the labeling laws for marijuana products in California are slightly different and more restrictive. As put forth by the 2020 California Code of Regulations (17, § 40410(g)), a supplier cannot put beer styles or beer terminology on cannabis beverage labels. The justification is that people may mistakenly assume that a label with a beer style descriptor implies that it is an alcoholic beverage.

As an aside, CERIA Brewing Company launched non-alcoholic cannabis beers in Colorado and in California, but had to use different labels in order to comply with each state's laws. It must be kept in mind that label changes are not inexpensive, and excessive costs can add up due to artwork changes, legal reviews, final printing, etc. In Colorado, CERIA's two styles of non-alcoholic beer are labeled as dealcoholized Belgian-style white ale and dealcoholized IPA (figs. 7.2 and 7.3). This allows consumers to know what styles of products are inside the cans before purchasing. Obviously, sampling of any cannabis products prior to purchase is strictly not allowed by law. In California, which has stricter labeling laws, the same two beers are labeled as "Grainwave Cannabis Infused Beverage" and "Indiewave Cannabis Infused Beverage." So, in California a supplier is handicapped by not being able to include the beer's style, and has to try to explain what the beverage is in the romance copy on the label, again without mentioning brewing terminology. The California label for CERIA Grainwave describes a "refreshing, medium-bodied beverage crafted with blood orange peel and coriander" (fig. 7.2). Note that the liquid is called a beverage, as the word "brewed" is not allowed since it is a brewing-related term. CERIA Indiewave is described as a "flavorful beverage that perfectly balances Cascade, Citra, and Amarillo hops with light caramel malt for a smooth citrus character" (fig. 7.3).

From these two descriptions a consumer in California must figure out what style of non-alcoholic beer they are purchasing and try to decide if the description fits the type of product they are looking for. Having one set of federal guidelines, as is the case with alcohol, would greatly simplify the work of suppliers who wish to distribute products in different states. However, depending on how a federal regulatory system is designed, states may still retain the independent right to impose their own labeling rules.

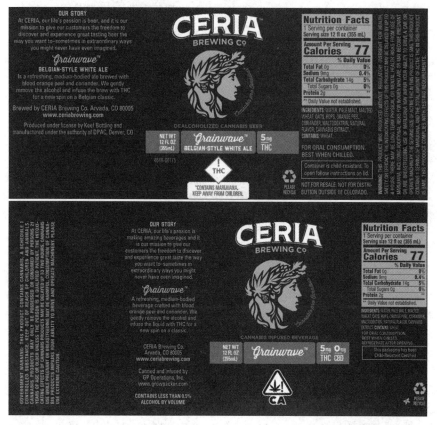

Figure 7.2. Comparison of labels on the cannabis beverage Grainwave for two different states, Colorado (*top*) and California (*bottom*).

Warning Labels

In addition to language requirements, beverages made with cannabis must carry a specific THC warning label. Similar to the standard alcohol warning label on beers, wines, and spirits, the THC warning must appear on the beverage label in a prominent manner that is on the front and centered to be highly visible. The THC warning labels for Colorado, California, Washington, and Michigan are examples of how states each have a unique labeling system (fig. 7.4). In the

Figure 7.3. Comparison of labels for the cannabis beverage Indiewave for two different states, Colorado (*top*) and California (*bottom*).

absence of federal legalization each state must create its own version of a THC warning label. Federal legalization will bring a warning label that is consistent state to state and is more easily recognized by adult cannabis consumers.

Figure 7.4. Mandated THC warning labels for selected US states. *Left to right*: Colorado, California, Washington, and Michigan.

Quality Considerations

In addition to a brewer's usual quality considerations, a marijuana-infused product must be measured for cannabinoid content to ensure it falls within the allowable limits. The product must also be treated to stabilize it since it is a food product. In other words, the beer must be pasteurized or be brewed to have low pH to avoid the growth of pathogens. Samples must be sent to state-approved laboratories for analysis to confirm that cannabinoid levels are within legal limits, and to check for microbial and other contamination, such as pesticides. Alcohol content is not routinely measured, but it must be less than 0.5% ABV. Regulators sometimes ask for analytical results.

Serving Size

A further note on marijuana products, specifically edibles and beverages, is serving size as it applies to the amount of THC per serving. This is required information that must be somewhere on the label. In general, most states that have legalized recreational marijuana have designated either 5 mg or 10 mg as a "standard" serving. Table 7.1 lists states where recreational marijuana was legal as of the end of 2020, showing standard serving sizes for THC in milligrams and the maximum THC content in a single edible retail product. Note that most states have a 100 mg maximum level for any single recreational marijuana product. Medical marijuana regulations allow for higher amounts, and at generally lower prices and tax rates.

Table 7.1 Standard serving size of THC by US state or district as of November 2020

State	Standard serving size, mg THC	Maximum THC content per single edible retail product, mg
Alaska	5	50
California	10	100
Colorado	10	100
District of Columbia	5	100
Illinois	10	100
Maine	10	100
Massachusetts	5	100
Michigan	10	100
Nevada	10	100
Oregon	5	50
Vermont	10	100
Washington	10	100

The National Advisory Council on Drug Abuse wanted to establish a standard serving for THC in order to have a more consistent way of measuring dosage during research studies. This would be similar to the "standard serving" of alcohol, which is usually considered to be 0.6 fl. oz. (or 14 g) of pure alcohol whether it comes from 12 fl. oz. of standard beer, 6 fl. oz. of wine, or 1 fl. oz. of distilled spirits.[4] The standard serving was recommended as 5 mg THC since this was the dose that led to observable intoxication in both beginning and experienced users without producing adverse reactions.

Federal Trademarks

When any company creates a logo or a new brand, normal business practice is to register it with the United States Patent and Trademark Office (USPTO) so that no other entity can use the logo or brand to promote its products. This is particularly useful when a brand becomes very successful. For example, Stone Brewing Company would not want any other brewery to use the name "Stone" on its beer packaging. In fact, Stone Brewing accused MolsonCoors of using the name "Stone" on its Keystone line of beers in a prominent manner, bringing a lawsuit in 2019 to protect its name and intellectual property. As with most lawsuits, many years will usually pass before complete resolution of disputes and the Stone Brewing case is no different.

In the world of cannabis, the federal government considers all products made with THC to be illegal, and therefore does not allow for them to be trademarked. To address this issue, many companies that make THC-containing products usually make a non-infused version of the same product and then sell it in the general market or online. Having demonstrated that the product was legally sold in interstate commerce, the company can then apply for trademark protection through the USPTO for the non-infused product. Then, the trademark granted to the non-infused product with the same name and logo is generally assumed to apply to the infused version, but this does not offer complete protection.

The USPTO has also made it clear that any non-drug products made with CBD cannot be trademarked, even if the CBD comes from hemp grown legally according to the Agriculture Improvement Act. This ruling came in 2020 from the Trademark Trial and Appeal Board. It is based on the FDA's

---

4   Nora D. Volkow, "Request for Information: Standard Unit Dose of THC," *Nora's Blog*, National Institute on Drug Abuse, March 23, 2020, https://www.drugabuse.gov/about-nida/noras-blog/2020/03/request-information-standard-unit-dose-thc.

decision to classify CBD as a drug during the initial testing of Epidiolex prior to 2018 (see p. 77). Since CBD was not previously recognized as a food supplement, the FDA decided that CBD should be treated as a drug and that any products made with CBD should also be classified as drugs. Accordingly, any food or beverages made with CBD cannot receive federal trademark protection at this time. However, any drugs made with CBD are allowed to apply for trademark protection. In the future, if the FDA determines that CBD is safe for use by the general public, then trademark protection is to be expected for non-medicine CBD products.

RECREATIONAL MARIJUANA PHYSICAL PACKAGING REGULATIONS

As with labeling, packaging requirements for marijuana products are more stringent than for alcoholic beverages. All beverages that contain legal recreational marijuana containing up to 10 mg THC per serving must be packaged with child-resistant ends (CRE). "Child resistant" generally means that a child of five years of age cannot figure out how to open the packaging. In contrast, an adult should be able to easily open the package. This means that typical aluminum cans with standard openings are not allowed because a child can quickly figure out how to pry open the tab with a finger. Examples of the types of closures that are allowed are the CAN+ end (fig. 7.5) or an XO "slider" end (fig. 7.6) or any other ends that have been successfully tested to be child resistant. Alternatively, bottles with modern twist-off bottle crowns are not allowed, again since a child can figure out how to twist it off. However, an old-style bottle crown that requires an opener (often referred to as a "church key") can be used because the law dictates that when a tool is required to open a package then it is, by nature, child proof.

Additionally, if a beverage contains more than 10 mg of THC up to the 100 mg THC maximum legally allowed for the recreational market, then the package has to be resealable and come with a measuring device to dispense a "standard" 10 mg serving. This is typical for the state of Colorado and several other states, such as Washington. With this requirement a carbonated beverage is not very practical, and a measuring device usually translates as a small plastic cup with graduation marks that is attached to the top of the container or glued to the underside of the cap, which usually does not look as attractive to consumers. Because of these limitations, this requirement almost always results in there being no carbonated beverages containing more than 10 mg THC per container sold in dispensaries.

In CERIA Brewing Company's experience, it is necessary to have a backup plan for CREs because of constant changes in the carbonated drinks market. CERIA started using the XO opener when getting into the cannabis market in 2018. The XO closure was fully approved for the state of Colorado and everything went smoothly. Several other cannabis beverage producers in Colorado also used the XO lid. However, in 2019 Mountain Dew® released a new product called Mtn Dew Amp Game Fuel®, which contained caffeine and other compounds to "improve accuracy and alertness." This product also advertised a resealable lid "designed for one-handed opening and closing—so you can power up while staying in the game." The new resealable lid was also billed as having "resealable tech" that "helps keep your Mtn Dew Game Fuel fresh and your hardware dry so you can focus on grinding."

Needless to say, the "resealable tech" was the XO lid, and Mountain Dew purchased virtually all available XO can ends in the US market for their new product. This left many cannabis beverage suppliers looking for an alternative CRE to use on their products. CERIA had looked at other lids previously and found the CAN+ lid to be adequate, but not as user-friendly as the XO lid. With no other choice, CERIA started using the CAN+ end in 2019. It was not until later in 2020 that the maker of XO ramped up production enough to start supplying the cannabis beverage industry with CREs once more. In the second half of 2020, CERIA switched back to the XO lid.

Fig 7.5. CAN+ end shown in black plastic compared to a traditional can end.

Figure 7.6. XO child-resistant end showing the closed position (*left*) and the open position (*right*). *Photo courtesy of Jody Villa.*

A unique packaging requirement for the state of Colorado is that edibles must be packaged in opaque packaging that prevents people from seeing the contents. For practical purposes, this means beverages should be in an aluminum bottle or aluminum can. Alternatively, glass or plastic bottles that have an opaque wrap can be used. In California, the law states that regular amber beer bottles are considered opaque when used for packaging cannabis beverages.[5] With this guidance, suppliers in California are free to use amber colored beer bottles with pry-open tops when packaging cannabis beverages. Most other states have similar packaging regulations—each supplier must consult legal guidance relevant to its state when packaging its products. As always, brewers should also consider the effects of light and oxygen on product quality and weigh those in their decision on how to package.

SALES TACTICS

Sales tactics when selling marijuana products are also subject to specific regulations. For one, any recreational marijuana product that contains THC must be sold in a licensed marijuana dispensary in those states where it is legal. Furthermore, any kind of sampling of marijuana products within dispensaries is illegal, even in states where medical and recreational marijuana are fully legalized. This is in stark contrast to alcoholic products, for which sampling is completely legal (within limits) in most states. In the cannabis market, if a supplier wishes to offer samples of its products, it must supply samples that are free of marijuana. Needless to say, it is very important that the product without marijuana should taste as close as possible to the flavor of the same product made with marijuana so that the consumer has a good idea of what they are purchasing.

Sampling promotions are closely watched by state cannabis regulatory authorities and must take place outside of the physical layout of the dispensary. This usually involves setting up a sampling booth in the parking lot or sidewalk in front of a dispensary and so weather becomes a factor. In Colorado, giving out merchandise, such as branded and logoed items, is usually permitted, but items should be of nominal value. In many ways this is similar to restrictions for alcoholic products, where it is sometimes illegal to give items above a certain level of value to consumers—the term "nominal value" is often used by state alcohol regulatory agencies—plus the items should bear substantial brand advertising and be small enough to be carried away by the consumer. Such items usually take the form of caps, t-shirts, stickers, and the like. Some states, such as California, do not allow any giveaways for cannabis-related products. Specific state regulations should be looked into before giving out promotional items.

---

[5]   Cal. Code Regs. tit. 17, § 40415(e) (2020).

Finally, in Colorado, authorities will not allow cannabis product suppliers to set up tents or banners with signage that displays any cannabis terminology or any images of cannabis that can be seen from publicly traveled streets, as this is viewed as outdoor advertising, which is prohibited. Violators are usually required to cover up offending images or words, or completely remove such signage, which can be a hardship if it is printed on a supplier's tent or other form of protection from the elements. Again, each state has different regulations regarding what is or is not allowed, and so competent legal advice should be obtained before attempting any type of advertising or promotional marketing.

SOCIAL MEDIA PROMOTION

An important part of modern marketing is to ensure a product's presence on social media. The consumer-packaged goods world is rife with hashtags and "@" symbols for "mentions" and daily posts on social networking services. At least one study has shown that 76% of consumers have purchased a product they have seen in a social media post, so marketers know that social media is a very effective platform.[6]

Products containing THC also have a social media presence, but in a different context since marijuana is still illegal under federal law. Most of the big social media platforms have community guidelines that specifically talk about posting anything that is illegal. As an example, Instagram's community guidelines under the "Follow the Law" section includes the following: "Offering sexual services, buying or selling firearms, alcohol, and tobacco products between private individuals, and buying or selling illegal or prescription drugs (even if legal in your region) are also not allowed." This rough guidance allows for most cannabis businesses to have social media accounts, but many such accounts have found themselves shut down (for obvious and not-so-obvious reasons) with or without warning. Companies in the business of selling cannabis products must tread a fine line. Do not attempt to second-guess social media providers or you risk losing access to their platforms.

Those accounts that get shut down can usually get up and running again within a couple of days after discussions between lawyers or representatives with good knowledge of the law. However, after restarting their online

---

6   Susan Gunelius, "How to Promote a Cannabis Business With Social Media Marketing," Cannabiz Media, May 8, 2020, https://cannabiz.media/how-to-promote-a-cannabis-business-with-social-media-marketing/.

accounts, businesses usually find that their long list of followers has been deleted. Therefore, many operators back up their list of followers frequently. In addition to daily backups of followers, many cannabis businesses are also careful to observe the following practices for social media accounts:

1. Never post prices, the $ symbol, or the % symbol. These seem to flag scanning software as potential indicators of illegal activity.

2. Never post the words *sale, discount, special, BOGO,* or other similar selling phrases as these are words that indicate a violation of the guidelines.

3. Avoid posts with images of a cannabis leaf or plant. Posts of product labels are usually tolerated, but pictures of cannabis leaves are sometimes all that is needed to justify a shutdown of the brand's online account.

4. Try to post the product in a positive social situation or in a scenic spot. Never post pictures of a person smoking cannabis or consuming a cannabis product. Any image that appears to promote consumption of an illegal product can lead to a warning letter or shutdown.

5. Posting a location or address may also lead to a warning letter or shutdown.

With these helpful hints in mind, there are still cannabis businesses that try to push the boundaries of what is allowable. However, most observe community guidelines and even try to act above the expectations of social media companies to show good corporate responsibility.

In conclusion, the reality is that the cannabis beverage industry and the alcoholic beverage industry are very different with regard to the regulations each must follow. The alcohol industry is well established and many of its regulations have been in place since the repeal of Prohibition in the early 1930s. Since the cannabis industry is so new, its regulations are evolving and clear guidelines for selling and marketing are not yet in place. Time, experience, legal studies, and federal legalization will help to tighten and clarify regulations so that future cannabis beverage suppliers are clear on what is and what is not allowed in this new industry.

8

METHODS OF MAKING NON-ALCOHOLIC CRAFT BEER

As mentioned in chapter 6, it is illegal to offer for sale alcohol and marijuana together in the same beverage in the US. Therefore, brewers must know how to produce beers without alcohol or how to remove alcohol from beers that contain it.

From a brewer's perspective, whether homebrewer or professional, balancing flavors in low- and no-alcohol beers to create products consumers desire is not an easy task. In fact, brewing flavorful non-alcoholic beers is arguably the most difficult path a craft brewer can choose because of the many issues that arise when alcohol is not part of the makeup of beer. The following discussion highlights the pros and cons of several methods of producing beer without alcohol. However, the first thing a brewer should realize is that the federal government has a classification system in place for beers based on alcohol content.

From a legal perspective, the Alcohol and Tobacco Tax and Trade Bureau (TTB) provides the following guidance to brewers who choose to produce low and non-alcoholic beers for sale in the US:[1]

- A malt beverage that is labeled as containing more than 0.5% alcohol by volume must not contain less than 0.5% alcohol by volume, regardless of any tolerance.
- Beers can be labeled as "low alcohol" and "reduced alcohol" if they contain less than 2.5% ABV but more than 0.5% ABV.
- Beers can be labeled as "non-alcoholic" if they contain less than 0.5% ABV, but this label must be accompanied by a clear statement that says "contains less than 0.5 percent alcohol by volume."
- Beers can be labeled as "alcohol free" if they contain no alcohol. A beer cannot be labeled as 0.0% ABV unless it is also accompanied by the "alcohol free" label. (See sidebar on p. 109 for how breweries use "0.0" as part of a product name to give the illusion they are 0.0% ABV.)

From these definitions it is clear that there are strict legal limits for alcohol content, within which brewers may apply their creativity to create products aimed at this particular segment of the beer market. Of course, this book does not constitute legal advice and so counsel should be retained to ensure proper labeling.

The second consideration for any brewer of non-alcoholic products is the presence of pathogenic microorganisms, which can harm humans. Some of the more infamous pathogens are *Escherichia coli*, *Listeria monocytogenes*, and *Clostridium* species. Fortunately, alcohol in beer inhibits the growth of pathogenic microorganisms. It is well documented that over the course of human history fermented alcoholic beverages were consumed by people of all ages for nutritional needs and because local water sources were unsafe to drink. In the absence of alcohol, pathogenic microorganisms were able to exist in beverages and resulted in human sickness and death. Even in today's modern brewing environment, beer without alcohol must be assumed to contain pathogens unless stabilized by suitable means. Several examples of acceptable stabilization include pasteurization, sterile filtration and the use of chemical preservatives (Hough et al. 1982, 715–722; Kunze 1996, 419). Any brewer choosing to offer non-alcoholic products is obligated to ensure their non-alcoholic beers are stabilized and fit for human consumption.

It should also be noted that if a brewery's non-alcoholic beer and other non-alcoholic beverage production constitutes more than 5% of the overall

---

[1] Alcoholic content, 27 C.F.R. § 7.71(c–f) (2012).

sales of the facility, the brewery must comply with all aspects of 21 C.F.R. §117 subparts C and G, which are Hazard Analysis and Risk-Based Preventive Controls and Supply-Chain Program, respectively.[2]

The methods of producing non-alcoholic beers can be separated into two types: biological, such as arrested fermentation or the use of specialty yeasts; and physical, including the use of thermal or membrane systems (Kunze 1996, 437–445).[3] Any method can be used by craft brewers, and each has its pros and cons. However, the ultimate choice with regard to producing a non-alcoholic beer will have to be made based on cost, taste, and technical expertise.

BIOLOGICAL METHODS

Arrested Fermentation

The most basic way to produce non-alcoholic beer is often referred to as arrested fermentation. In this method, the brewer simply stops the fermentation at a point when the desired alcohol level is achieved. This type of fermentation is usually carried out at low temperatures to help slow the fermentative activity of the yeast. A lager yeast is generally employed in arrested fermentation because an ale yeast at low temperatures will tend to fall out of suspension and cease fermentative growth. When the desired alcohol level is achieved the yeast is separated from the wort. In theory, arrested fermentation is very straightforward and can achieve levels below 0.5% ABV. The main drawback of arrested fermentation is that a worty, slightly sweet flavor persists into the finished beer, which is not unexpected since the yeast is not allowed to ferment all of the sugars present in the wort. This is why it is important to have as much cold contact time with the yeast as possible in order to impart flavor with limited alcohol production.

To help address flavor issues, the brewer will typically prepare wort with a lower original gravity compared to the alcoholic version of the same beer, usually targeting a starting gravity that is close to the desired final gravity, allowing for maximum fermentation of about 0.9°P (about 3 gravity points). A hot mash, that is, one greater than 158°F (70°C), also helps to limit the presence of fermentable sugars. Of course, if the fermentation results in a final alcohol content greater than 0.5% ABV, the brewer will have to dilute the product with sterile wort or de-aerated water until it is less than 0.5% in

---

[2] Exemptions, 21 C.F.R. §117.5(i)(2)(ii) (2021).

[3] Mike Tysarczyk, "Can any brewery compete in growing non-alcohol sector?" First Key, accessed February 10, 2021, https://firstkey.com/can-any-brewery-compete-in-growing-non-alcohol-sector/.

order to label it as non-alcoholic. The starting gravity will also dictate the level of body and sweetness in the final product and so 10°P (1.040 SG) or lower is usually advised in order to minimize malt sweetness. Some brewers also increase bitterness and hop flavor to help mask the sweet wort taste. Finally, many brewers add food-grade acid to lower the pH from between 5.0 and 5.5 (i.e., typical of wort) to between 4.0 and 4.5 (i.e., typical of beer). The other challenge with arrested fermentation is that there is still a good amount of fermentable material present so the final product must be stabilized, preferably by pasteurization. Another type of arrested fermentation that has been studied is continuous fermentation with high concentrations of immobilized yeast. It is unlikely that a craft brewer would use this method because of the high level of technical expertise required, as well as the cost and time investment.

Specialty Yeasts

Another method to produce non-alcoholic beer is to utilize microorganisms that are incapable of fermenting certain sugars. As maltose is the most common sugar in brewer's wort, yeasts with limited or no ability to ferment this disaccharide have been the object of recent studies. Some of these yeasts include *Saccharomycodes ludwigii*, *Pichia kluyveri*, *Zygosaccharomyces rouxii*, and *Torula delbrueckii*. Although these yeasts are capable of producing low-alcohol products, the main issue is that the flavor-active compounds (e.g., esters, higher alcohols, and organic acids) produced by these yeasts are slightly different to those produced by a standard brewer's yeast. Thus, the flavor profile of the finished product will be different compared to that of a standard brewer's yeast. The other drawback is that, like any brewery that uses different yeast strains, a separate yeast handling system is needed to avoid cross contamination.

When using a yeast that produces low-alcohol beer, pitching rates are generally low, and the wort glucose level is kept low to minimize fermentation activity. A mash profile is usually employed that optimizes β-amylase activity to produce as much maltose as possible. Additionally, a brewer's adjunct syrup with high maltose content can be used to supplement the wort. Depending on the amount of glucose present, the final alcohol content can be in the range 0.5%–1.5% ABV but may be as low as 0.1%. As with arrested fermentation, the final product will have to be stabilized in order to prevent contamination by pathogens and possible further alcohol production from contaminating yeasts.

PHYSICAL METHODS

Physical methods of producing non-alcoholic beer involve allowing fermentation to go to completion and then removing alcohol from the finished beer. Physical methods result in arguably better-tasting products compared to the biological methods described in the previous section. A brewer should consider that potable alcohol is obtained as a by-product of these physical methods and can range in strength from 30% to 80% ABV. Since many beers are around 5% ABV, a theoretical 100-barrel batch (117.3 hL) will yield about 155 gallons (587 L) of pure alcohol. This by-product can be diluted with water and flushed down the drain in accordance with local disposal guidelines, or it can be recovered. Hypothetically, the collected alcohol can be sold to help offset the cost of the dealcoholizing system. It can be sold as a craft spirit, such as beer schnapps; it can be used to create prepackaged craft cocktails; it can be sold to a craft distiller who is in need of supplemental alcohol; or it can be sold to oil companies to be used as fuel alcohol. Proper licensing, including obtaining a distiller's permit from the TTB, will need to take place if the brewer chooses to capture alcohol from the dealcoholizing unit. Finally, insurance and fire codes will need to be researched to make sure that alcohol storage is allowed on the brewer's premises.

The equipment required for the physical removal of alcohol can be expensive and usually involves copious engineering and space planning. Costs can easily be in the hundreds of thousands of dollars. Some dealcoholizers have smaller footprints than others but, regardless of size, placement is critical because it needs various utilities such as steam, clean-in-place (CIP), carbon dioxide, air, and water. Production outputs can range from a few barrels of dealcoholized beer per hour to over one hundred barrels per hour. There are two main ways to achieve alcohol removal: membrane methods and thermal methods.

Membrane Methods

There are two membrane methods that can be used for alcohol removal by brewers, which are dialysis and reverse osmosis. The advantage of both of these methods is that low temperatures are used instead of heat, thus limiting the loss of fresh flavor. However, there are some drawbacks. Neither method can realistically remove the alcohol down to zero, so production of alcohol-free beer is not practical. Additionally, dialysis can be expensive because the membranes require replacing about every five years. Plus, beer is usually required to be filtered prior to running through a dialysis membrane and so cloudy, yeasty beers cannot be processed. Finally, typical CIP chemicals found in breweries may damage dialysis membranes and so a separate CIP system is usually required.

For the majority of craft breweries who want to use a membrane to remove alcohol, reverse osmosis (RO) is more practical. An RO system involves using high pressure (about 40 bar, or 4 MPa) to force liquid through a membrane that is only permeable to small molecules (water and ethanol). Larger molecules, like flavor and aroma compounds, cannot pass through the membrane, so these are left behind in the beer. This phase is referred to as the dialysis filtration phase. In the final phase—the redilution phase—de-aerated, de-ionized water is added to the beer to replace the water and ethanol that were removed during the filtration phase until the volume of the beer is the same as the volume at the start of the process. At the end of the process, the beer will contain less than 0.5% alcohol by volume. It is obviously necessary to have a source of de-aerated, de-ionized water to run an RO system.

Thermal Methods

There are two main thermal methods that can be used to dealcoholize beer: evaporation and vacuum distillation. However, evaporation techniques, such as falling film evaporators and spinning cone column evaporation, are rarely, if at all, used in modern breweries.

Vacuum distillation, also known as vacuum rectification, is the thermal method used in modern breweries. Mention of "distillation" brings fear to most brewers, who know that heating beer is bad for quality. However, brewing research in Germany during the 1990s found that the boiling point of alcohol in beer for dealcoholization can be decreased significantly when the beer is in a vacuum. Under standard laboratory conditions the boiling point of alcohol is 173°F (78°C). However, when alcohol is placed in a vacuum it boils at around 104°F (40°C), thus minimizing the presence of "cooked" flavors in the final beer. In addition, it was found that many flavor-active compounds, such as esters and higher alcohols, also boiled off at low temperatures under vacuum and could be captured and dosed back into the finished, dealcoholized beer to improve the flavor (Kunze 1996, 441–443). This newfound knowledge resulted in a wave of non-alcoholic beers introduced to the European market that had flavor similar to alcoholic beer. Finally, vacuum distillation was found to reliably achieve products with alcohol levels below 0.05% ABV, which could be labeled as alcohol-free. It should be noted that the alcohol-free beer market is especially important to some customers for religious reasons.

Alcohol Free Labeling

As helpful as the TTB can be in some instances, they have not been very clear in regard to the definition of "alcohol free." Lawyers and representatives from CERIA have spoken with TTB personnel on different occasions and have received different answers. Sometimes TTB rulings can be difficult to interpret. Many laboratory personnel know that it is exceedingly difficult to measure a beer with 0.00% alcohol, even with modern alcohol measuring equipment. A sample containing 0.00% alcohol can register readings ranging from −0.02% to 0.02% ABV. A negative reading is technically false, but the equipment does not know this. To further complicate things, some countries in Europe allow the label to read "alcohol free" for any beers containing less than 0.5% ABV, which must be labeled as "non-alcoholic" in the US.

A couple of large international brewers apparently solved this dilemma by labeling their alcohol-free beers with the numerals 0.0 in the name, that is, "Name of Beer 0.0," then formally labeling the primary package as "Non-Alcoholic Beer with <0.5% ABV." Thus, no claim to be 0.0% ABV is made.

REMOVING ALCOHOL FROM HOMEBREW BEER

For many homebrewers who want to produce non-alcoholic beers, the only practical option at this point in time is to use heating to remove alcohol. There seems to be no real agreed upon parameters as to how much time this takes on a homebrew scale, so proceed with that in mind. When a brew is complete, the next step after aging/maturation/conditioning (which should be carried out in the presence of living yeast and alcohol for optimum results) is to place the brew back into the brew kettle and heat it to 173°F (78°C), either on a stovetop or in an oven, to boil off the alcohol. Make sure that adequate ventilation is present to avoid the buildup of ethanol fumes. Holding the brew at 173°F in an oven is easier to control versus using an open flame, but make sure that the oven is properly vented to avoid buildup of ethanol fumes. A typical homebrew five-gallon batch at 5% ABV will contain 32 fl. oz. of ethanol (equivalent to 50 mL ethanol per liter). The time it takes to boil off all of this alcohol differs markedly depending on where you look. Some sources report that a typical five-gallon batch should be held at 173°F (78°C) for 15–30 minutes to remove the majority of alcohol.[4] In these cases, the final alcohol content was not measured. It is possible that the authors guessed at the level of alcohol by smelling the aroma and concluded that the majority of alcohol

---

[4] See John Naleszkiewicz, "Brew a Great Non-Alcoholic Beer," *Brew Your Own* (October, 1995), https://byo.com/article/brew-a-great-non-alcoholic-beer/; and "How to Make Non-Alcoholic Beer," Midwest Supplies, October 25, 2019, https://www.midwestsupplies.com/blogs/bottled-knowledge /how-do-you-make-non-alcoholic-beer.

was boiled off when the aroma of alcohol in the vapor diminished. Or they wanted to minimize the formation of off-flavors due to heating and so stopped after 15–30 minutes. The US Department of Agriculture's report on nutrient retention factors indicates a much longer time is needed to completely remove the alcohol from foods cooked with alcohol.[5] A chart from this report has data showing approximately 2.5 hours is needed to get down to 0.5% ABV. Of course, this data is for a controlled experiment with a stirred alcohol beverage, and so the true hold time is probably somewhere in between. After holding at 173°F (78°C) for the required time, the brew should be cooled immediately and stored as cold as possible but taking care to stay above 32°F (0°C) since the absence of alcohol will mean the beer freezes at the same temperature as water. It should be noted that removal of alcohol by heating is similar to pasteurization and so the resulting "pasteurized" non-alcoholic beer will have to be handled in a sterile manner to avoid contamination from microorganisms that would normally be inhibited by the presence of alcohol.

Finally, if removing alcohol by holding beer at 173°F (78°C), note that the bitterness will be increased due to additional isomerization of residual hop alpha acids. It is recommended that hopping rates are lowered to compensate for this and avoid obtaining a final product that is intensely bitter.

---

[5]   Nutrient Data Laboratory, *USDA Table of Nutrient Retention Factors: Release 6* (U.S. Department of Agriculture, December 2007), https://data.nal.usda.gov/system/files/retn06.pdf.

9

CANNABIS BEER RECIPES

PROCESSED MARIJUANA IN BREWING

Cannabinoid Decarboxylation

One of the most important aspects about brewing with marijuana is to ensure that the desired cannabinoids have become fully activated. In other words, CBD and the psychoactive compound THC both exist in the marijuana plant as the carboxylic acid precursors CBDA and non-psychoactive THCA, respectively. The usual way in which to activate them is to decarboxylate them (i.e., remove the acid portion) using heat, which converts them into CBD and THC.

Temperatures for decarboxylating cannabinoids were studied quite thoroughly by Wang et al. (2016). It was found that temperatures up to 293°F (145°C) can be used, with hotter temperatures resulting in faster conversions. At 293°F complete decarboxylation occurs in as little as six minutes.

Table 9.1 shows the time for complete conversion in relation to temperature. It should be noted that the vaporization temperature of THCA is 220°F (104°C), so a sealed pressure-rated container should be used to avoid excessive losses of this THC precursor.

Table 9.1 Time required for decarboxylation of THCA to THC at various temperatures

Temperature		Time to 100% decarboxylation of THCA to THC
°F	°C	Minutes
203	95	60[a]
230	110	30
266	130	9
293	145	6

Source: Wang et al. (2016), *Cannabis and Cannabinoid Research* 1(1): 262–271.
[a] Note that 203°F (95°C) results in 90% conversion after 60 minutes.

There are several practical options for heating cannabis to decarboxylate THC. Mechanical decarboxylators can be readily purchased, such as the Ardent FX unit (https://ardentcannabis.com/product/nova-fx/), and precision laboratory heating and drying ovens are available from suppliers like Thermo Fisher Scientific. Alternatively, a regular kitchen oven can also be used.

Prior to decarboxylation, the cannabis plant material should be soaked in cold water for three to four hours to remove chlorophyll compounds that can result in off-flavors, and then allowed to dry thoroughly (see "Processing Marijuana Shake for Brewing" later in this chapter on p. 122).

When adding decarboxylated cannabis material to a brew for dry hopping, it is best to use a nylon net to act as a "tea bag," in the same way most small-scale brewers do with hops. These nets, or hop sacks, are inexpensive and can be easily obtained from most homebrew shops.

Estimating THC when Adding Marijuana to Beer

In terms of quantity of marijuana to use, a good starting point is 0.1 oz. per 5 gal. of brew (0.15 g/L). How strong of a brew this becomes will largely depend on the strength of the cannabis material used. It is best to use this starting point and then adjust the amount used in future brews to find the desired end point. With experience using their process and knowing typical losses, plus increasing familiarity with the strength of cannabis material they are using, a brewer can devise a simple spreadsheet calculator to target the

THC dose per bottle:

1. Cell ① contains the known percent THC dry weight (e.g., 22%, or 0.22).
2. Cell ② contains the desired ounces of marijuana to use per brew (e.g., 0.1 oz.).
3. Cell ③ contains the total brew volume in fluid ounces (nb. 1 US gallon equals 128 fl. oz.). A typical 5 gal. batch is 640 fl. oz.
4. Cell ④ contains the estimated efficiency for THC through-out the process (e.g., 33%, or 0.33).
5. Cell ⑤ calculates the total milligrams of THC per brew, which is cell ② multiplied by 28349.5 (mg per ounce), then multiplied by cell ①.
6. Cell ⑥ calculates the total milligrams of THC per brew after losses, which is cell ⑤ multiplied by cell ④.
7. Cell ⑦ calculates milligrams of THC per 12 fl. oz. bottle, which is cell ⑥ divided by cell ③, then multiplied by 12.

The steps above can be condensed into the following formula:

$$\text{mg THC per 12 oz. bottle} = \frac{(\text{oz. marijuana} \times 28349.5 \times \%\text{THC dwt.} \times \%\text{THC eff.})}{(\text{total brew vol. in fl. oz.})} \times 12$$

With the above example, and assuming only 33% efficiency, it can be seen that each 12-ounce bottle should have 3.86 mg of THC, which is about half the typical serving size of THC for edibles and drinkables. Again, the brewer can choose to move the THC target higher or lower, depending on their experience level and tolerance.

Shake and Trim

Different parts of the cannabis plant have different levels of THCA, which is the precursor to THC. As discussed earlier, the THCA must be converted, or decarboxylated, to the psychoactive form THC. Some strains have buds with potential THC levels higher than 30%. Stems, however, usually contain about 1% THC but can be as high as 9% THC.[1] Stems also do not appear to contain any other cannabinoids except for cannabinol (CBN), which is the

---

[1] Jonathan Wani, "What's in The Stems?" MCR Labs, November 20, 2014, https://mcrlabs.com /resources-post/whats-in-the-stems/.

breakdown product of THC. This knowledge is important for marijuana processors who extract THC because it converts a waste stream into a value-added product in the process. The industry term for stems and other leftovers from processing is *shake*.

Another industry leftover is *trim*, which consists of the small leaves, called sugar leaves, that are trimmed away from the buds of a mature cannabis plant in order to make the harvested buds look as good as possible in dispensaries (see p. 29). Trim is often classified into four grades according to quality and content of cannabinoids, with grade 1 being the highest quality and grade 4 the lowest.[2] The THC content of trim can range from 5% to 15% when using grades 1–3. Grade 4 is usually avoided due to its very low, if any, THC content and the presence of foreign debris. This grading system is useful to brewers so that they can search out grades 1–3 for use in beers but avoid grade 4.

CHOOSING HOW TO ADD MARIJUANA

Cannabis can be added to a brew either on the hot side or cold side. Both types of additions can achieve brews that contain THC and lead to intoxication or other desired effects. At smaller scales, such as a 5-gallon homebrew batch, both methods are financially feasible. However, if you intend to make larger volumes, you should take the following factors into consideration: the cannabis source and cost; the form of cannabis when it is added; and the ability to extract THC from the cannabis into the beer during the brewing process.

Cannabis source and cost are critical when scaling up because the cost of buds can be prohibitive, typically costing US$100 to US$300 per ounce depending on the quality and THC content. In other words, cost of goods sold (COGS) for cannabis alone can run from US$600 to US$1,800 per barrel (US$512–$1,535 per hL), which translates to an additional cost of about US$2.40–$7.26 per pint (16 fl. oz.). In general, this is financially prohibitive for the majority of craft brewers. In contrast, if a brewer has a source of low-cost shake or trim then COGS is reduced considerably. A typical industry price for shake and trim in 2020 ranged from US$150 to US$400 per pound (US$330–$880 per kilo), depending on the quality. This translates to an additional cost of US$56–$150 per barrel (US$48–$128

---

2   "How to Make Cannabis Oil from Trim," extraktLAB, accessed November 30, 2020, https://extraktlab.com/how-to-make-cannabis-oil/.

per hL), which is still expensive but more palatable than buying buds. In fact, additions of other rare ingredients to beer can rival this cost.

The form of cannabis should also be taken into consideration, as it can be added as buds, shake/trim, or extract. It is most cost-effective to perform in-house extractions of shake and trim rather than purchasing commercial extract. It is also more cost-effective to extract shake and trim instead of brewing with it because its low THC content means a relatively large addition of plant material is needed, which can possibly introduce off-flavors.

There are several efficient methods to prepare cannabinoid extractions from cannabis material. Those involving highly flammable solvents, such as butane, should be avoided unless performed by a trained chemist in a laboratory designed for work with explosive materials. Butane is a non-polar solvent, and so is extremely efficient at extracting cannabinoids and terpenes without extracting other plant compounds such as chlorophyll. However, every trace of butane must be removed from the extract by a trained chemist to avoid fires, explosions, and solvent entering the food chain.

The safer alternative, compared to butane, is to produce a tincture using alcohol as the solvent for extraction. This method is preferable since THC and other cannabinoids are readily soluble in alcohol (ethanol), and it is relatively easy to obtain potable spirits from reputable sources. One drawback is that alcohol also extracts other plant materials, such as chlorophyll and waxes. Another disadvantage is that high-proof spirits (i.e., those greater than 70% ABV) are best for extraction but these happen to be highly flammable. In addition to ensuring that the alcohol is high proof, it is important that it is clean. In other words, it should not contain flavors or sweeteners. So, flavored high-alcohol spirits should be avoided. Food-grade grain neutral spirits (another name for pure, neutral-tasting alcohol) at 95% ABV are ideal to use for extraction. The following method results in satisfactory extraction of cannabinoids into a tincture.[3] This method can make about one pint (roughly 475 mL) of cannabis extract, but it can be scaled up to make large quantities if desired and where this is legal.

---

[3]   Glenn Panik, "How to Make Marijuana Tincture (Decarboxylation & Alcohol Extraction of THC and CBD)," *Cannabis Growing*, March 3, 2013, https://cannabisgrowing.blog/2013/03/03/how-to-make-marijuana-tincture-decarboxylation-alcohol-extraction-of-thc-and-cbd/.

How to Make a Cannabis Tincture

Note: To avoid the extraction of unwanted matter, the plant material should be soaked in cold water for three to four hours. Detailed steps are on page 122 in the section Processing Marijuana Shake for Brewing. The plant material should then be allowed to dry thoroughly before extraction.

1. Place 1.0 oz. (28.3 g) marijuana material, finely ground for best extraction, into a sealable glass container, such as a glass French square.

2. Pour in 16 fl. oz. (0.475 L) of grain neutral spirits greater than 70% ABV and mix thoroughly.

3. Seal the glass container and shake for 30 seconds.

4. Store the container at room temperature for 48 hours, shaking occasionally to expose as much material to the alcohol as possible.

5. After 48 hours, the alcohol/cannabis mixture is filtered through food-grade cotton cloth or similar filter material into a clean glass container. Any residual liquid contained in the filter media is squeezed out into the glass container to collect as much cannabis tincture as possible.

6. The resulting cannabis tincture will have a dark color due to the extraction of chlorophyll and other plant material (if not previously soaked to remove it), but it is very rich in cannabinoids. The concentration of THC in the tincture can be calculated by knowing the starting percentage content THC of marijuana material, weight of material, and final tincture volume. The tincture should be transferred into brown glass bottles for storage and dosing.

7. Store in cool, dark conditions for a shelf life of approximately one year.

Hot Side Addition

Since cannabis and hops are "cousins" (see chap. 2), it has been theorized that cannabis can be added to the brew kettle in the same manner as hop additions during the boil. The heat should convert (decarboxylate) the THC from its non-psychoactive form to its psychoactive form during the boil, similar to the way that the heat from boiling isomerizes hop alpha acids. A 60-minute kettle boil is indeed enough to decarboxylate more than 90% of the THCA into THC (see table 9.1, p. 114). In addition, a brew kettle boil is not adequate to boil off the critical cannabinoids of the marijuana plant, as THC and CBD at standard pressure do not vaporize below 300°F (149°C).[4]

However, as easy as hot side addition sounds, it is not recommended because of estimated losses of cannabis compounds. It is expected that cannabis compounds will experience losses similar to hop compounds during the brewing process. For example, hop bitterness can be expected to see losses from 24.7% to 41.54% from boiling to packaging (Popescu et al. 2013, 115). These losses can be attributed to incomplete isomerization of alpha acids, adhesion of bitterness compounds to the tank walls, entrainment with trub, and loss through filtration. Additionally, isomerized alpha acids are known to adhere to the cell walls of yeast, which leads to further losses.

At the present time, we should assume that losses of THC will occur throughout the brewing process if cannabis is added during the boil. THC is known to be extremely hydrophobic and should be expected to react in brewing situations in a similar manner to hop alpha acids, which means substantial losses of THC and other hydrophobic or volatile compounds. In a typical 50 bbl. craft brewhouse, this loss could be 40% of the typical cost of US$100 per bbl. for shake, resulting in a total loss of about US$2,000 per brew.

Cold Side Addition

Given the high THC losses from hot side additions of cannabis, cold side additions are the safer and more cost-effective alternative. There are two forms of cold side addition: adding decarboxylated cannabis in the same manner as dry hopping (dry potting!); and addition of decarboxylated cannabis extract, generally added to the finished product prior to packaging. The addition of extract is analogous to the addition of pre-isomerized hop extracts to post-fermented beer that some brewers use to ensure bitterness targets are achieved.

It is important to note that any cold side additions of cannabis must use decarboxylated material in which the THC is fully activated, as explained in the opening section of this chapter. Even if the finished product is packaged and pasteurized, a typical beer pasteurization regime of about 20 pasteurization units (PUs) is not enough to fully activate THC.[5] The process for decarboxylating THC in cannabis is not difficult but there are several steps that should be followed closely to obtain the best results.

---

[4]   Anthony Franciosi, "Vaping Temperature Chart: The Complete Guide," Honest Marijuana Co., accessed November 30, 2020, https://honestmarijuana.com/vaping-temperature-chart/.

[5]   1 PU is defined as one minute at 140°F (60°C).

NOTES ON THE RECIPES

If I had to sum up the following brewing recipes, it would be to say that brewing is part science and part art. It is hoped that after reading through the efforts of these boundary-breaking brewers, any avid brewer will be keen to replicate and then expand the knowledge base of brewing with marijuana. Perhaps creative brewers may find a novel way of decarboxylating THC that is faster or easier, or they might find a better way of extracting cannabinoids from plant material that is safe and efficient. Maybe even one of you reading this will develop a rapid beer aging procedure that involves low-temperature cannabinoid extraction at the pH of beer.

Many of the following recipes have been curated from out-of-print sources or the internet. In their original form, not all of these recipes provided all of the information that modern brewers and homebrewers might be used to documenting. Specifics such as original gravity (OG), final gravity (FG), estimated international bitterness units (IBUs), hop alpha acids, water profiles, and specific yeast strains—to name a few—may not have been mentioned. In these cases, assumptions were made using best guesses based on professional and homebrewing experience. In such instances, I have marked these values as "author estimate." Bittering hop alpha acid contents were generally estimated at 10%. Where hop varieties were not specified, I did not want to presume and give specific suggestions. For the older recipes, it is hard to know exactly what hops were available. Back in the 1990s, hops were available mainly according to what the big brewers dictated they would buy. So, Hallertau, Tradition, and Perle were readily available as late addition hops (aroma), and Chinook, Columbus, and Galena, for example, were available for bittering. Modern hop varieties certainly have "dank" qualities that would be well suited to pairing with cannabis.

The amount of THC actually extracted and decarboxylated from cannabis at the pH and alcohol concentration of the beer, and over the course of several days remains an unknown quantity, so one can only guess at the amounts. Since hop bittering compound losses have been reported to be as low as 40%, but typically are as much as 60% which means an extraction efficiency of 40%, we can be pretty safe in assuming that the process of making cannabis beer is less efficient and that only 30% of THC is extracted and decarboxylated if non-activated marijuana is added to the brew during the course of the brewing process. Thus, a 30% efficiency will be assumed in the following recipes unless noted otherwise.

RECIPES FROM *MARIJUANA BEER*

Although stories and rumors abound that the founding fathers grew can-nabis and smoked and brewed with it, historians say this was not the case. In fact, America's first president grew hemp, but nowhere did George Washington mention in his journals that he smoked it or brewed with it (Lee 2012, 17). Rather, he grew hemp for seed and fiber so that he was not reliant on hemp from Europe. One of the first documented sources of beer made with cannabis is a 1996 book entitled *Marijuana Beer: How to Make Your Own Hi-Brew Beer* by Ed Rosenthal and the Unknown Brewer (2nd ed., Oakland: Quick American Archives). It is easy to understand why the Unknown Brewer moniker was used in a published book during the 1990s when cannabis was illegal throughout the United States. In spite of this, Ed Rosenthal revealed to the public a small treasure trove of valuable cannabis research regarding brewing.

Unlike buds, which are the most valuable part of the plant because the majority of THC is concentrated in them, shake is typically regarded as waste by marijuana processors because of flavor issues or perceived quality prob-lems. As we saw earlier (pp. 115–116), however, the leaves and stems that comprise marijuana shake can contain anywhere from 1% to 9% THC by dry weight. One of Rosenthal's most important insights was that these plant parts that were regarded as waste in the cannabis industry could be used effectively as brewing adjuncts. It remains unknown whether the shake in the *Marijuana Beer* recipes was activated, that is, decarboxylated. Most likely it was not, since the role of decarboxylation was not studied until well after the 1990s (Wang et al. 2016). Rosenthal found that using shake was financially feasible and good enough quality to use when brewing beers where an equivalent amount of bud would have been prohibitively expensive (Rosenthal and Unknown Brewer 1996, 18). Interestingly, because it does not appear to contain any additional cannabinoids other than CBN and THC, shake is an almost perfect ingredi-ent to use in brewing from a cost perspective as it can mimic or replace the intoxicating effects of alcohol.

It is important to note that these recipes may not reflect best practices, cur-rent science, or otherwise fall in line with homebrew practices that we use today. The brewing process as described in *Marijuana Beer* was a means to an end, using beer as the delivery system. Use your best judgement after read-ing the recipes through and apply your homebrewing knowledge. The recipes below are presented as a historical reference and to encourage your creativity when diving into the world of brewing with cannabis.

What a difference 20 years makes! The THC content in the 1990s averaged around 4%. With the 1996 legalization of medical weed in California, companies were eager to develop stronger strains. Selective breeding and improved cultivating techniques raised the average THC content by 2014 to about 12% (Mahmoud et al. 2016, 613). In 2020 there were even reports of some strains that were even higher, up to 20% THC. So it is important to note these increases in THC before making the recipes below since they were made with marijuana that had 1990s levels of THC.

The marijuana shake preparation and the six beer recipes that follow in this section are adapted from *Marijuana Beer* (Rosenthal and Unknown Brewer, 1996). The book is currently out of print, but Rosenthal has granted permission for the recipes to be adapted and reproduced here.

PROCESSING MARIJUANA SHAKE FOR BREWING

Ed Rosenthal found that brewing with unprocessed marijuana shake led to off-tastes in beer because of the marijuana's water-soluble components (e.g., chlorophyll, tannins, etc.). In order to alleviate these off-flavors, he outlined in *Marijuana Beer* the following series of steps to prepare marijuana shake for using it in brewing:

1. Weigh out the desired amount of marijuana plant material for a homebrew batch.
2. Place the marijuana in a nylon mesh bag and place the filled nylon mesh bag in a large pot.
3. Add lukewarm water to the pot and allow the bag to soak for one hour. Do not use hot water to avoid leaching oils from the plant material.
4. Remove the bag from the pot and gently squeeze to remove water.
5. Repeat the soaking process three to four times. Soaking removes water-soluble tannins and chlorophyll.
6. Before discarding the soak water, inspect the bottom of the pot for any glandular trichomes that have separated from the marijuana. If present, collect these cannabinoid-rich glands by pouring off the water carefully and then rinsing and drying them. The trichomes can be smoked, but care should be taken since they are a potent source of cannabinoids.
7. Rinse the marijuana a final time. Allow to dry. This processed marijuana can now be used in the recipes that follow.

SIMPLE HEAD ALE
5 gallons (19 L)

OG: 1.052

FG: 1.009

SRM: Depends on color of malt extract

IBU: 30 IBU [author estimate]

ABV: 6% ABV

MALTS AND FERMENTABLES
7.25 lb. (3.29 kg) hopped liquid malt extract, either light, amber, or dark

HOPS
(Uses hopped malt extract.)

CANNABIS
5–7.5 oz. (142–213 g) processed marijuana shake [see Author Commentary]

WATER
Drinking water to top up extract to 5 gal. (19 L)

YEAST
1 packet ale yeast [unspecified, see Brewing Notes]

ADDITIONAL ITEMS
5.25–7 oz. (149–198 g) corn sugar for priming

BREWING NOTES
1. Pour malt extract into fermentation vessel.
2. Fill vessel with boiling water to 5 gal. (19 L).
3. Allow to cool to less than 80°F (27°C).
4. Add packet of ale yeast.
5. Cover vessel with lid and air lock.
6. Ferment at 55–80°F (13–27°C) until complete, usually up to 2 weeks. [Author's comment: recommend using Chico yeast strain and fermenting at 60–72°F, 16–22°C.]
7. Add processed marijuana to fermentor 2–3 days before bottling.
8. For bottling, rack beer off the sediment and plant material, then dissolve priming sugar in hot water and mix into the beer.
9. Bottle into cleaned bottles and crown.
10. Age at 68–72°F (20–22°C) for several weeks before drinking.

AUTHOR COMMENTARY

The original recipe did not give any estimate of bitterness, so I have assumed 30 IBU in the finished beer. There were some specific notes on extract gravity given, from which we can deduce some information. Many brewing syrups are typically concentrated to 75–85 degrees Brix to increase the osmotic pressure and inhibit growth of microorganisms. We can assume that the malt extract had a starting concentration at the high end of 85 degrees Brix, which is equivalent to 85 g of sucrose per 100 g of solution. The degrees Brix scale is almost identical to the Plato scale used in brewing, and so the starting gravity is almost equivalent to 85°P. We know that 7.25 lb. of malt extract has a volume of about 0.756 gallons, and so when 0.756 gallons is put into a final volume of 5 gallons of water, there will be a 6.614-fold dilution. Hence, the starting 85°P would be diluted 6.614-fold to 12.9°P. This is roughly in accordance with the 1.052 OG that was stated in the original. No aeration of the wort was mentioned. Since we do not know the amount of yeast cells added but we do know that the fermentation completed at 1.009 FG, it is likely that the nutritional needs of the yeast were adequately met.

With a name like Simple Head Ale, we can assume this recipe produces a golden pale ale with 6% ABV and moderate bitterness of 30 IBU. This would definitely be an easy drinking beer with a good hop bitterness for balance. The only potential issue with this recipe is the addition of 5–7.5 oz. of shake specified in the original. If we assume an addition of 6 oz. of 1990's shake at about 1.2% THC (the mean of THC concentrations reported in shake at that time) and 33% efficiency throughout the process, we end up with about 12.6 mg of THC per 12-ounce bottle.[6] This would be a bit high for a typical beer drinker. Although this would be slightly strong for a novice user, those with high tolerance levels would most likely find this level of THC to be effective and pleasant.

One suggestion for improvement would be to decarboxylate the shake prior to adding to the fermentation vessel to ensure that all of the THCA is converted to THC. The amount of shake added could then be reduced. It is unknown to what extent decarboxylation took place in this and the following recipes, but since the author of *Marijuana Beer* is a renowned cannabis expert it is assumed that some active THC was present in the final product.

---

[6]   Jonathan Wani, "What's in The Stems?" MCR Labs, November 20, 2014, https://mcrlabs.com/resources-post/whats-in-the-stems/.

HOP HEAD BEER
5 gallons (19 L)

OG: 1.054

FG: 1.007

SRM: Depends on color of malt extract

IBU: 80–90 [author estimate]

ABV: 6.1%

MALTS AND FERMENTABLES

4 lb. (1.81 kg) dry malt extract, light, amber, or dark

2 lb. (0.91 kg) sugar

HOPS

2.5 oz. (71 g) bittering hops

1 oz. (28 g) aroma hops

CANNABIS

5–7.5 oz. (142–213 g) processed marijuana shake

WATER

Drinking water to make up to 5 gallons

YEAST

One packet of ale yeast

BREWING NOTES

1. Dissolve DME in 5 gallons (19 L) water.
2. Bring to a boil and add bittering hops.
3. Boil 40 minutes.
4. Add crystal malt.
5. Boil 20 minutes.
6. Remove from heat.
7. Add priming sugar and aroma hops.
8. Transfer to fermentation vessel and allow to cool to less than 80°F (27°C).
9. Add packet of ale yeast.
10. Cover vessel with lid and air lock.
11. Ferment at 55–80°F (13–27°C) until complete, usually up to 2 weeks. [Author's comment: recommend using Chico yeast strain and fermenting at 60–72°F, 16–22°C.]

12. Add processed marijuana to fermentor 2–3 days before bottling.
13. For bottling, rack beer off the sediment and plant material, then dissolve priming sugar in hot water and mix into the beer.
14. Bottle into cleaned bottles and crown.
15. Age at 68–72°F (20–22°C) for several weeks before drinking.

AUTHOR COMMENTARY

Compared to Simple Head Ale (p. 123), the Hop Head Beer recipe goes a little further in lightening up the malt character while increasing the hops. The ratio of malt to sugar adjunct for this beer is 2:1, which is similar to modern, mainstream lagers. Additionally, using light, amber, or dark malt will lead to flavors ranging from a light, biscuity taste to roasty, coffee-like flavors.

Regarding bitterness, we might assume that the original bittering hops used were about 10% alpha acid and were boiled for 60 minutes. Final IBUs would have been between 80 and 90, depending on brewing conditions. The late hops would have added negligible bitterness as they appeared to be in the wort for a very short time, but they would have added a decent amount of hop aroma to the finished beer. A couple of complimentary hop varieties to consider adding would be Columbus, Summit, and Nugget to highlight the dank aroma of cannabis. Assuming the marijuana shake would have been 1.2% THC (similar to that in the recipe for Simple Head Ale), this would result in about 12.6 mg THC per 12-ounce bottle, but bear in mind the higher THC content of many modern cannabis strains. Overall, this recipe will produce a light-bodied ale with light malt character, an assertive bitterness, a warming alcohol sensation, and a dry finish. The combination of alcohol and THC might be a bit much for a beginning user, but should be a bitter, tasty treat for a user with more experience. One suggestion for improving this beer is to decrease the bittering hop addition to bring the IBUs down, and to decarboxylate the shake.

POT-PALE ALE
5 gallons (19 L)

OG: 1.051
FG: 1.009
SRM: Amber colored

IBU: 50–60 [author estimate]
ABV: 6.1% [author estimate is 5.4%]

MALTS AND FERMENTABLES
6 lb. (2.72 kg) light dry malt extract
0.5 lb. (0.23 kg) sugar [author comment: probably dextrose]
1.5 lb. (0.68 kg) British crystal malt

HOPS
1.5 oz. (43 g) bittering hops

CANNABIS
5–7.5 oz. (142–213 g) processed marijuana shake

WATER
Drinking water to fill to 5 gallons (19 L)

YEAST
1 packet ale yeast

BREWING NOTES
1. Dissolve DME in 5 gallons (19 L) water.
2. Bring to a boil and add bittering hops.
3. Boil 40 minutes.
4. Add crystal malt.
5. Boil 20 minutes.
6. Remove from heat.
7. Add priming sugar and aroma hops.
8. Transfer to fermentation vessel and allow to cool to less than 80°F (27°C).
9. Add packet of ale yeast.
10. Cover vessel with lid and air lock.
11. Ferment at 55–80°F (13–27°C) until complete, usually up to 2 weeks. [Author's comment: recommend using Chico yeast strain and fermenting at 60–72°F, 16–22°C.]

12. Add processed marijuana to fermentor 2–3 days before bottling.
13. For bottling, rack beer off the sediment and plant material, then dissolve priming sugar in hot water and mix into the beer.
14. Bottle into cleaned bottles and crown.
15. Age at 68–72°F (20–22°C) for several weeks before drinking.

AUTHOR COMMENTARY

The hop addition would have given between 50 and 60 IBUs. As before, estimating the THC content of 1990s cannabis material, the THC per 12-ounce bottle would have been about 12.6 mg. Overall, this recipe will produce a flavorful brew with caramel notes and medium body, the assertive bitterness of a pale ale, and a buzz-worthy amount of alcohol and THC. The caramel provides balance for the bitterness and makes for a very drinkable beer.

POTTED PORTER
5 gallons (19 L)

OG: 1.052
FG: 1.009
SRM: Dark brown to black
[author estimate]

IBU: 80–90 [author estimate]
ABV: 6.1%

MALTS AND FERMENTABLES
5 lb. (2.27 kg) light dry malt extract
2 lb. (0.91 kg) dark dry malt extract
0.5 lb. (0.23 kg) crystal malt
0.5 lb. (0.23 kg) black patent malt

HOPS
2.5 oz. (71 g) bittering hops
1 oz. (28 g) aroma hops

CANNABIS
5–7.5 oz. (142–213 g) processed marijuana shake

WATER
Drinking water to fill to 5 gallons (19 L)

YEAST
1 packet ale yeast

ADDITIONAL ITEMS
4.3 oz–5.3 oz. (122–150 g) priming sugar

BREWING NOTES
1. Add dry malt extracts to 2 gallons (7.57 L) boiling water to dissolve any clumps.
2. Continue boiling for 40 minutes
3. Add crystal malt, black patent malt and bittering hops. Top off to 5 gallons.
4. Boil 20 minutes.
5. Remove from heat.
6. Add aroma hops.

7. Cool to less than 80°F (27°C), add yeast, and cover vessel with lid and air lock.
8. Ferment at 55–80°F (13–27°C) until complete, usually up to 2 weeks [author's comment: recommend using Chico yeast strain and fermenting at 60–72°F, 16–22°C].
9. Add processed marijuana to fermentor 2–3 days before bottling.
10. For bottling, rack beer off the sediment and plant material. Then, dissolve priming sugar in hot water and mix into the beer.
11. Bottle into cleaned bottles and crown.
12. Age at 68–72°F (20–22°C) for several weeks before drinking.

AUTHOR COMMENTARY

In this recipe, the two malt extracts and two malts result in a very dark colored beer, which is expected for a porter. A half pound of black patent adds a roasty, ashy taste, but it is tempered by the crystal malt and light malt extract in the malt bill. This beer has a rich body with a lot of dark flavors appropriate for the style. With 2.5 oz. of bittering hops, the final IBU was in the 80–90 range, making for an assertive bitter finish. The 1 oz. of late hops adds a nice, light hop aroma that helps balance the dark malt aromas. With a final alcohol content of about 6.1% ABV, the result is a medium-to-full-bodied porter with plenty of bitterness from the hops and dark malts. With an estimated THC content of about 12.6 mg per 12-ounce bottle, this brew would be great to sip in the evening. One suggestion for improvement would be to decrease the bittering hop dose to about half (40–45 IBU) so the perceived bitterness would be a bit more balanced, since there would be some malt bitterness coming from the use of black patent malt.

LIGHT-HEADED LAGER
5 gallons (19 L)

OG: 1.050   **IBU:** 8–12 [author estimate]

FG: 1.007   **ABV:** 6%

SRM: Pale [author estimate]

MALTS AND FERMENTABLES
6 lb. (2.72 kg) light, hopped dry malt extract

1 lb. (0.45 kg) corn sugar

HOPS
(Uses hopped malt extract.)

CANNABIS
5–7.5 oz. (142–213 g) processed marijuana shake

WATER
Drinking water to fill to 5 gallons (19 L)

YEAST
1 packet lager yeast

ADDITIONAL ITEMS
5.25 oz. (149 g) priming sugar

BREWING NOTES
1. Add dry malt extract to 2 gallons (7.57 L) boiling water.
2. Continue boiling for 40 minutes.
3. Add corn sugar and top off to five gallons, and boil further 20 minutes.
4. Remove from heat and cool to less than 80°F (27°C).
5. Add 1 packet lager yeast, cover vessel with lid and air lock.
6. Ferment at 45–60°F (7–16°C) until complete, usually three to four weeks.
7. After fermentation is complete, transfer beer to a clean vessel with airlock.
8. Age at 33–40°F (0.6–4.4°C) for 4–8 weeks.
9. Add marijuana 2–3 days before bottling.

10. For bottling, dissolve priming sugar in hot water and mix into the fermentor.
11. Bottle into cleaned bottles and cap.
12. Age at 68–72°F (20–22°C) for several weeks before drinking.

AUTHOR COMMENTARY

With 14% of the fermentables being adjunct, this lager would have a light body and pale color. The hop aroma would be mostly absent, while bitterness would be low, maybe around 10 IBU. With 12.6 mg of THC per 12-ounce bottle, this will make for a refreshing, light lager with a strong buzz. One suggestion for improvement is to decrease the THC target by half to 5.5 mg/12-ounce bottle. This would give a really nice thirst-quenching beer, of which a couple could be enjoyed on a hot day.

HEADWISER
5 gallons (19 L)

OG: 1.051
FG: 1.008
SRM: Pale [author estimate]

IBU: 45–55 [author estimate]
ABV: 5.9%

MALTS AND FERMENTABLES
5 lb. (2.27 kg) light malt extract
1.5 lb. (0.68 kg) flaked rice
1.5 lb. (0.68 kg) corn sugar

HOPS
1.5 oz. (43 g) bittering hops
0.5 oz. (14 g) aroma hops

CANNABIS
5–7.5 oz. (142–213 g) processed marijuana shake

WATER
Drinking water to fill to 5 gallons (19 L)

YEAST
1 packet lager yeast

ADDITIONAL ITEMS
5.25–7 oz. (149–198 g) priming sugar

BREWING NOTES
1. Add malt extract and flaked rice to 2 gallons (7.57 L) water.
2. Heat to 150°F (66°C) for 40 minutes.
3. Add water to adjust volume to 3 gallons (11.4 L).
4. Remove flaked rice.
5. Add bittering hops and top off to five gallons and boil for 20 minutes.
6. Remove from heat, then add sugar and aroma hops.
7. Strain wort through cheesecloth.
8. Add 1 packet lager yeast, cover vessel with lid and air lock.
9. Ferment at 45–60°F (7–16°C) until complete, usually three to four weeks.

10. After fermentation is complete, transfer beer to a clean vessel with airlock.
11. Age at 33–40°F (0.6–4.4°C) for 4–8 weeks.
12. Add marijuana 2–3 days before bottling.
13. For bottling, dissolve priming sugar in hot water and mix into the fermentor.
14. Bottle into cleaned bottles and cap.
15. Age at 68–72°F (20–22°C) for several weeks before drinking.

AUTHOR COMMENTARY

This very light-colored beer is interesting because of the light flavor and moderate bitterness. Assuming the rice flakes were uncooked adjunct, the 150°F hold probably resulted in no starch breakdown since the canned malt extract specified had no diastatic activity. Also, the rice flakes will lighten the color of the brew even more than expected from light malt extract alone, but also result in a haze that cheesecloth cannot readily remove. The moderate body should be very good at complimenting the moderate bitterness of about 50 IBU. The 11 mg of THC contributed by the marijuana shake will make for an interesting beer to drink, with a deceptively light color, moderate body, moderate bitterness, but a hefty buzz.

A couple of suggestions are to swap out the rice flakes for dextrose to lighten the body for more drinkability, or include a small amount of ground pale malt to provide the proper enzymes to break down the starch from the rice flakes. Also, the bitterness and THC targets should be cut in half to make for a quaffable light beer that a person can drink more than one of and still feel good.

Overall, the previous six recipes from *Marijuana Beer* provide a good view of how a person in the 1990s would have gone about making homebrews with cannabis. Obviously, homebrewing knowledge and techniques were perhaps simpler than those of today, but the resulting products were usually flavorful and drinkable.

RECIPES FROM BREWERS FRIEND

Whereas the recipes from *Marijuana Beer* represent recipes from a time when extract brewing was prevalent, modern homebrewing has become much more advanced. This is showcased in the following four recipes curated from Brewers Friend (https://www.brewersfriend.com), a popular brewing website. It should be noted that the first two recipes use marijuana, whereas the last two use hemp. However, marijuana and hemp can be swapped or mixed in the recipes to obtain the brewer's desired effect.

BRUHAHA BELGIAN-STYLE TRIPEL WITH THC

Original recipe by Jones Bros. - C. Ashlin; B. & B. Jones (December 6, 2019)

5 gallons (19 L)

OG: 1.075 (18.2°P) **IBU:** 43

FG: 1.010 (2.56°P) **ABV:** 8.6%

SRM: 6

MALT AND FERMENTABLES

5 lb. (2.27 kg) Belgian Pilsner malt

3.75 lb. (1.7 kg) dry malt extract – Pilsner

0.63 lb. (0.29 kg) wildflower honey

1.25 lb. (0.57 kg) clear Belgian candi sugar

0.94 lb. (0.43 kg) Belgian biscuit malt

HOPS

1.25 oz. (35 g) Target (5.5% AA) @ 60 min.

0.5 oz. (14 g) Cascade (5.5% AA) @ 60 min.

2.5 oz. (71 g) Saaz (2.5% AA) @ 10 min.

CANNABIS

14.4 fl. oz. (425 mL) THC tincture (see Brewing Notes)

WATER

5 gallons (19 L) distilled water for mashing

1.88 gallons (7.1 L) distilled water for sparging

YEAST

Mangrove Jack's Belgian Tripel M31

ADDITIONAL ITEMS

0.63 oz. (18 g) crushed coriander

BREWING NOTES

THC tincture (see also Author Commentary)

Soak trim leaves and small buds in 60% ABV spirit in a Mason jar. Heat to 120°F (49°C) for 120 minutes, then store for 2 months, with weekly agitation by hand.

Brewing the beer

1. Add malts, honey, and sugar to 5 gallons (19 L) mash water.
2. Mash at 150°F (66°C) for 60 minutes.
3. Sparge with 1.88 gallons (7.1 L) water at 170°F (77°C).
4. Bring to boil and add Target and Cascade hops at start of boil.
5. Add Saaz hops and coriander 10 minutes before end of boil.
6. Remove from heat.
7. Add sugar when wort is down to 100°F (38°C). [Author comment: typically, adjuncts should be added in the boil to ensure proper sanitization.]
8. Add honey at 75°F (24°C), immediately prior to adding yeast. [Author comment: Adding honey at this temperature will preserve more flavor, but there is a risk of contamination.]
9. Ferment at 65°F (18°C) for two days.
10. Increase fermentation temperature to 68°F (20°C) and allow to ferment five more days.
11. Transfer to secondary and age at 68°F (20°C) for two weeks.
12. Add 14.4 fl. oz. (425 mL) of THC tincture to the 5-gallon batch immediately before adding 155 oz. (4,394 g) sucrose priming sugar. This batch doses and primes the beer prior to packaging.

AUTHOR COMMENTARY

This recipe makes for a very fine tasting and authentic Belgian-style tripel, especially with 16% adjunct in the fermentables to lighten up the body. The bitterness and hop selection are very appropriate for the style.

My only suggestion for improvement is the preparation of the THC tincture. The best alcohol to use for tinctures is 95% ABV spirit (p. 118). This recipe calls for 60% ABV, which is good but not ideal for extraction. Moreover, the decarboxylation step should be at a hotter temperature to ensure all of the THCA is converted to the active form of THC. We can see from table 9.1 that the lowest temperature studied by Wang et al. (2016) was 203°F (95°C), which achieved 90% conversion after 1 hour. If the data from table 9.1 were extrapolated out to 120°F (49°C), it would take 223 minutes to obtain active THC. This means that the original tincture recipe likely only converted little more than half of the THCA to THC. Since the variety and the potential THC content of the buds and trim was not given, and the weight of these materials was also missing, it is very difficult to estimate the final THC of each bottle. However, it is probable that a small amount of THC was present in the Belgian-style tripel made, and at 8.6% ABV a very enjoyable time was probably had by all.

CANNABIS IPA

Original recipe by Brewer #248371 [Karol] (July 24th, 2019)

5 gallons (19 L)

OG: 1.046   **IBU:** 42.18
FG: 1.011   **ABV:** 4.63%
SRM: 4.46

MALT AND FERMENTABLES

6.2 lb. (2.8 kg) Briess LME Golden Light Malt Extract

HOPS

0.6 oz. (17 g) Simcoe (12.5% AA) @ 60 min.
0.6 oz. (17 g) Simcoe (12.5% AA) @ 30 min.
0.44 oz. (13 g) Eureka (18% AA) @ 15 min.

CANNABIS

1.47 oz. (41.7 g) cannabis

WATER

6 gallons (23 L) distilled water

YEAST

Mangrove Jack's Liberty Bell Ale M36

BREWING NOTES

1. Add light malt extract to 2.4 gal. (9.1 L) distilled water and bring to boil.
2. Add 0.6 oz. (17 g) Simcoe hops at start of boil.
3. After 30 minutes of boiling, add 0.6 oz (17 g) Simcoe hops.
4. After 45 minutes of boiling, add Eureka hops.
5. At end of boil, allow to cool to 63–73°F (17–23°C).
6. Add distilled water to increase volume to 5 gallons (19 L).
7. Pitch yeast at 0.35 million cells/mL/°P.
8. Add cannabis and allow to rest in primary for 10 days, fermenting at 63–73°F (17–23°C).
9. Carbonate to 2.25 vol. CO_2 and then bottle.

AUTHOR'S COMMENTARY

This recipe results in a lighter, more sessionable IPA with decent hop aromas from late hopping in the kettle. The addition of a hefty amount of cannabis, presumably buds, would add considerable cost and THC to the final product. Ensure the cannabis material remains completely submerged to avoid mold forming. It is estimated that each 12-ounce bottle would contain about 57 mg THC, which is quite strong for the average consumer. Additionally, the aroma from cannabis terpenes will probably overpower any hop aromas because the cannabis is added as a dry pot in primary versus all the hop additions being added during the boil. You might consider preparing a tea with the cannabis material instead, although this was reported to yield a barely noticeable aroma in the beer (Karol, pers. comm.). Overall, this brew is recommended only for those cannabis users who can tolerate high doses. New users with lower tolerance should avoid this recipe.

HEMPNOTIC WEIZENBOCK

Original recipe by 10 Palms [Sean Parker] (April 7, 2017)

5 gallons (19 L)

OG: 1.076 (18.4°P)   **IBU:** 18 IBU

FG: 1.019 (4.8°P)   **ABV:** 7.5%

SRM: 21 SRM

MALT AND FERMENTABLES

8 lb. (3.63 kg) American Wheat malt

2.5 lb. (1.13 kg) American Pilsner malt

2.25 lb. (1.02 kg) American Munich malt 20L

1.0 lb. (0.45 kg) German Caramunich III malt

0.5 lb. (0.23 kg) German melanoidin malt

0.5 lb. (0.23 kg) Belgian Special B malt

0.13 lb. (0.06 kg) German Carafa I malt

0.5 lb. (0.23 kg) rice hulls

HOPS

1 oz. (28 g) Hallertau Mittelfruh (3.75% AA) @ 60 min.

1 oz. (28 g) Tettnanger (5.3% AA) @ 5 min.

CANNABIS

8 oz. (227 g) hemp hearts

16 oz. (454 g) hemp seeds

YEAST

White Labs – WLP300 Hefeweizen Ale Yeast

BREWING NOTES

1. Mash in milled malts, rice hulls, and hemp hearts at 1.5 qt./lb. (3.13 L/kg).
2. Hold 60 minutes at 152°F (67°C).
3. Boil 60 minutes, adding Hallertau Mittelfruh hops and hemp seeds at start of boil.
4. Add Tettnanger hops 5 minutes before end of boil.
5. Remove from heat and cool to 62°F (17°C).
6. Pitch yeast at 0.5 million cells/ml/°P.
7. Ferment to completion at 70°F (21°C)
8. Bottle at 2.7 vol. CO_2.

AUTHOR COMMENTARY

This 52% wheat brew is a bold expression of the style, but still within the guidelines of a weizenbock. The addition of hemp hearts and hemp seeds is very hefty and will contribute a lot of fatty acids. Hemp seeds refer to the complete dried seed, and hemp hearts refer to the hulled seed without the outer shell. Neither hemp seeds nor hemp hearts contain cannabinoids. The recipe does not indicate if the seeds were roasted, so it is assumed that they were not and so should not contribute much to the flavor of the finished beer except for a light hemp, grassy flavor. The fatty acid contribution will have benefited the yeast to the point where the yeast crop was likely several times larger than normal. Overall, this will produce a strong and deliciously sippable brew for a cold winter's night.

HEMP BROWN ALE

Original recipe by David Swaciak, Franklinstein Brewing (March 18, 2017)

5 gallons (19 L)

OG: 1.057 (14.04°P) **IBU:** 22

FG: 1.013 (3.32°P) **ABV:** 5.7%

SRM: 16

MALT AND FERMENTABLES

9 lb. (4.08 kg) American 2-row pale malt

1.0 lb. (0.454 kg) German Munich light malt

1.0 lb. (0.454 kg) American caramel 60

0.63 lb. (0.29 kg) American malted hemp seeds

HOPS

0.5 oz. (14 g) Cascade (7% AA) @ 30 min.

0.7 oz. (20 g) Cascade (7% AA) @ 10 min.

CANNABIS

3 oz. (85.0 g) hemp

WATER

Ca 60 ppm, Mg 5 ppm, Na 10 ppm, SO_4 55 ppm, Cl 95 ppm, HCO_3 0 ppm

YEAST

White Labs – WLP007 Dry English Ale Yeast

ADDITIONAL ITEMS

0.10 oz. (2.95 g) calcium chloride (anhydrous)

0.12 oz. (3.54 g) Epsom salts

BREWING NOTES

1. Mash in malts, brewing salts, and malted hemp seeds at 1.32 qt./lb. (2.71 L/kg) at 151°F (66°C) for 60 minutes.
2. Sparge with 3.25 gallons (12.3 L) of 170°F (77°C) water.
3. Boil for 60 minutes, adding 0.5 oz. (14 g) Cascade hops after 30 minutes and 0.7 oz. (20 g) Cascade hops 10 minutes before end of boil.
4. Remove from heat and cool wort to 72°F (22°C).

5. Add hemp to primary fermentor.
6. Pitch yeast at 0.35 million cells/mL/°P.
7. Ferment at 72°F (22°C) to completion.
8. Package at 2.75 vols. CO_2 [Author comment: assume the beer is racked off of the plant material prior to packaging].

AUTHOR COMMENTARY

Overall, this recipe will create a nice brown ale with potentially a high amount of cannabinoids from the addition of hemp. Of course, assuming industrial hemp was used at an upper THC content of 0.29% by dry weight, then this recipe could have as high as 1.5 mg THC per 12-ounce bottle, even assuming an efficiency of 33% during the fermenting process. Ensure that the hemp is added during primary fermentation so that it is utilized by the yeast and issues with head retention in the finished beer are avoided. The oils in hemp seed will provide the yeast with nutrients to build cell membranes and multiply, much like the addition of oxygen. The final yeast crop will be about five times that of a normal yeast crop.

Overall, this will be a great beer to drink, with rich flavors of lightly kilned malts to enjoy along with, perhaps, some calming effects from the cannabinoids, especially THC, at a microdose level. This is a brew even novice cannabis users can enjoy.

AUTHOR RECIPES

Being a professional brewer for over 30 years, and a homebrewer for 6 years prior to that, has allowed me ample opportunity for experimentation with brewing ingredients, processes, and equipment. Obtaining a doctoral degree in brewing science from the University of Brussels in Belgium led me down the path of questioning all that is known about brewing, and to the realization that there is still much more to discover. When thinking of such critical questioning, there are two examples (out of many) that come to mind. What is the maximum amount of wheat that a brewer is able to use in a wheat beer? And, is the process of the light-struck reaction in beer reversible? What follows are background stories and the recipes that resulted, which I invite homebrewers to recreate.

All-Wheat Lager

As a young PhD brewer in 1995, I had the opportunity to meet many fellow brewers around the world who had multiple years of experience. Being interested in wheat beers, my first question to many of them had to do with the maximum amount of wheat that could be used in a brewing recipe. Almost without hesitation, the majority reiterated the classic brewing textbook explanation that 60%–70% is the maximum that should be used to avoid lautering problems. Probing further as to whether a beer made from 100% wheat was possible, the answer was a resounding "No," which I translated as "Possibly." In an effort to study this issue, I found there are a few potential problems that arise when using 100% wheat, the critical one being filtration issues in the brewhouse. An all-wheat brew has the very real possibility of clogging a lauter tun or a mash filter press. A clogged lauter tun or mash filter press may also lead to poor runoff, which leads to poor yield and low gravity. In the 1990s, the solution to brewing an all-wheat ale with a lauter tun was to incorporate rice hulls to help set the filter bed, and to keep plenty of brewing enzymes handy to add in an emergency, especially enzymes like heat-stable α-amylase and Laminex® (a mixture of β-glucanases and xylanases), which decrease viscosity and improve filtration efficiency. Both enzyme products are available at homebrew shops. A mash filter did not require rice hulls, which was quite unexpected, and actually worked fairly problem-free with an all-wheat mash, even though brewing enzymes were kept on hand in case of a stuck mash. With this in mind, the following is a recipe for an all-wheat lager that is infused with cannabis and has a smooth body with a clean finish. Brewing enzymes should be added to the mash tun at the first sign of a stuck mash; use the amount as indicated in the supplier's instructions.

ALL-WHEAT LAGER
5 gallons (19 L)

OG: 1.046 (11.4°P)	**IBU:** 11
FG: 1.008 (2°P)	**ABV:** 5.0%
SRM: 5	

MALT AND FERMENTABLES
7 lb. (3.18 kg) malted white wheat
1 lb. (0.45 kg) rice hulls

HOPS
0.17 oz. (4.9 g) Nelson Sauvin (12% AA) @ 60 min.

CANNABIS
0.06 oz. (1.7 g) of decarboxylated buds at 22% THC @ dry hop

YEAST
SafLager – W-34/70

ADDITIONAL ITEMS
0.07 oz. (2 g) Laminex @ mash in
0.08 oz. (2.4 g) calcium chloride (dihydrate) @ 60 min.
1 tablet Whirlfloc® @ 10 min.
0.002 oz. (0.06 g) zinc sulfate heptahydrate (22.7% zinc) @ 5 min.

BREWING NOTES
1. Mash in malted wheat and rice hulls at 1.32 qt./lb. (2.71 L/kg) and Laminex at 113°F (45°C). Hold at 113°F (45°C) for 30 minutes.
2. Raise to 126°F (52°C) and hold for 25 minutes.
3. Raise to 149°F (65°C) and hold for 45 minutes.
4. Raise to 167°F (75°C) and hold for 10 minutes for mash out conversion.
5. Sparge with 170°F (77°C) water to kettle full volume of 5.3 gallons (20 L).
6. Boil for 60 minutes, adding 0.17 oz. (4.9 g) Nelson Sauvin hops and calcium chloride at start of boil.
7. Add Whirlfloc tablet 10 minutes before flameout.
8. Add zinc sulfate 5 minutes before flameout.

9. Remove from heat and whirlpool for 10 minutes, then rest for 20 minutes.
10. Adjust post-boil volume to 5 gallons (18.9 L), if boiloff was excessive.
11. Cool wort to 54°F (12°C) and pitch W-34/70 yeast at 1 million cells/ml/°P.
12. Ferment at 54°F (12°C) to completion, then rack to aging vessel.
13. Drop temperature to 39°F (4°C), add cannabis, and age until diacetyl is not detected (usually 2–3 weeks).
14. Package at 2.7 vols. CO_2.

AUTHOR COMMENTARY

This recipe results in a very smooth, easy-to-drink all-wheat beer. The addition of decarboxylated cannabis adds about 5 mg THC per 12-ounce bottle after process losses of about 20%. The THC adds about 2 perceived IBUs for a nice bitterness that balances out the malty wheat flavor. The combination of 5% ABV plus 5 mg THC gives a relaxing feeling and allows the user to enjoy a couple without getting full. This All-Wheat Lager recipe makes a great beer to drink on its own, or it can be the base for other types of malt beverages. For example, the clean flavor permits the brewer to add fruits or herbs, even those with delicate flavor profiles such as peach or lavender. The flavors come out without being overwhelmed by barley malt or other strong flavors. Additionally, this all-wheat base can be very useful for making clean-flavored, malt-based seltzers. Adding dextrose adjunct, up to 50%, will provide a lighter colored malt beverage with an even cleaner finish to create flavorful hard seltzers. Finally, running this base through a carbon filter will effectively remove most of the color and flavor to create an even cleaner base.

1970s Summertime Lager

The question of the light-struck reaction in beer has been bothersome because it is basically a sulfur-based problem, which should be correctable. However, many brewing scientists who have written and lectured about the reaction and its deleterious effect on beer have stated the presence of the skunky off-flavor is enough to discard bottles or whole batches of beer. After I retired, my daughter and I talked about how copper is used by distillers and vintners to clean up sulfurous notes in their respective products. Since the light-struck off-flavor in beer caused by 3-methyl-2-butene-1-thiol

(3MBT) is sulfurous in nature, we decided to test if copper ions had the ability to clean up the skunkiness. A series of tests involving beer with and without the addition of copper gluconate and exposed to direct sunlight proved that the sensory aspect of the light-struck reaction is preventable and reversible (Villa and Villa 2020). With this in mind, what follows is a recipe for a 1970s-type American lager that can be consumed by the glassful in direct sunlight. I picked the 1970s because most domestic lagers during that decade were about 5% ABV and 18–20 IBUs, which resulted in very flavorful, drinkable beers.

1970S SUMMERTIME LAGER
5 gallons (19 L)

OG: 1.046 (11.4°P)   **IBU:** 18
FG: 1.010 (2.5°P)   **ABV:** 4.7%
SRM: 3

MALTS AND FERMENTABLES
5 lb. (2.27 kg) pale malt, 2-row
2 lb. (0.9 kg) flaked rice

HOPS
0.32 oz. (9 g) Hallertau Hersbrucker (4.5% AA) @ 60 min.
0.43 oz. (12 g) Hallertau Mittelfruh (5% AA) @ 60 min.
0.32 oz. (9 g) Cascade (6% AA) @ 15 min.

CANNABIS
0.06 oz. (1.7 g) of decarboxylated buds at 22% THC @ dry hop

YEAST
Wyeast – 2247-PC European Lager

ADDITIONAL ITEMS
1 tablet Whirlfloc @ 10 min.
0.07 oz. (2 g) zinc sulfate heptahydrate (22.7% zinc) @ 5 min.
1 ml copper gluconate 0.5 M solution @ package
[Copper gluconate supplements are available from health food stores.]

BREWING NOTES
1. Mash in pale malt and flaked rice at 1.32 qt./lb. (2.71 L/kg) at 140°F (60°C). Hold at 140°F (60°C) for 30 minutes.
2. Raise to 151°F (66°C) and hold for 60 minutes.
3. Raise to 167°F (75°C) and hold for 10 minutes for mash out conversion.
4. Sparge with 170°F (77°C) water to kettle full volume of 5.3 gallons (20 L).
5. Boil for 60 minutes, adding 0.32 oz. (9 g) Hallertau Hersbrucker and 0.43 oz. (12 g) Hallertau Mittelfruh hops at start of boil.

6. Add 0.32 oz. (9 g) Cascade hops 15 minutes before flameout.
7. Add Whirlfloc tablet 10 minutes before flameout.
8. Add zinc sulfate 5 minutes before flameout.
9. Whirlpool for 10 minutes and rest for 20 minutes.
10. Adjust post-boil volume to 5 gallons (18.9 L), if boiloff was excessive.
11. Cool wort to 54°F (12°C) and pitch Wyeast 2247 yeast at 1 million cells/ml/°P.
12. Ferment at 48°F (9°C) to completion, then rack to aging vessel.
13. Drop temperature to 39°F (4°C), add cannabis, and age until diacetyl is not detected (usually 2–3 weeks).
14. Prior to packaging, add 1 ml of 0.5 M copper gluconate solution to the fermenting vessel and swirl gently to mix.
15. Package at 2.7 vols. CO_2.

AUTHOR COMMENTARY

This recipe results in a flavorful, drinkable beer with a 1970s attitude. The addition of decarboxylated cannabis adds about 5 mg THC per 12-ounce bottle after process losses of about 20%. The THC adds about 2 perceived IBUs for a nice bitterness that is similar to the lagers of the 1970s. The light alcohol and THC give a relaxing feeling. The addition of copper will act to bind up any sulfurous light-struck aroma compounds when the beer is exposed to light. This beer can be enjoyed on the beach or by the pool while soaking up the sun.

One final note: copper can decrease the shelf life of beer due to heavy metal oxidation, so the shelf life will not be as long as beer without copper.

Non-Alcoholic Stout and Porter

Stout is a style of beer that is always enjoyable but can easily be made decadent by adding the right ingredients. The following recipe is a rich stout that can be enjoyed slowly after dinner.

Porter is a great style of beer that goes well with the taste of roasted peanuts found in peanut butter. The porter recipe that follows below has a combination of flavors, especially peanut butter and chocolate, that makes for a great dessert beer.

NA CHOCOLATE COCONUT CREAM STOUT
Non-alcoholic milk stout with marijuana

5 gallons (19 L)

OG: 1.057 (14°P) **IBU:** 30
FG: 1.014 (3.5°P) **ABV:** <0.5%
SRM: 70

MALTS AND FERMENTABLES
6.5 lb. (2.9 kg) pale malt, 2-row
2 lb. (0.9 kg) Munich malt
1 lb. (0.45 kg) caramel 60°L
0.5 lb. (0.23 kg) chocolate malt
1 lb. (0.45 kg) lactose

HOPS
0.64 oz. (18 g) Fuggle (5% AA) @ 60 min.
0.64 oz. (18 g) Willamette (5.5% AA) @ 60 min.

CANNABIS
0.2 oz. (5.7 g) of decarboxylated buds at 22% THC

YEAST
White Labs – WLP004 Irish Ale Yeast

ADDITIONAL ITEMS
4 oz. (113 g) cacao nibs @ 60 min.
7 oz. (200 g) toasted coconut @ 10 min.
1 tablet Whirlfloc @ 10 min.

BREWING NOTES
1. Mash in malts and lactose at 1.32 qt./lb. (2.71 L/kg) at 140°F (60°C). Hold at 140°F (60°C) for 30 minutes.
2. Raise to 154°F (68°C) and hold for 10 minutes.
3. Raise to 167°F (75°C) and hold for 10 minutes for mash out conversion.
4. Sparge with 170°F (77°C) water to kettle full volume of 5.3 gallons (20 L).
5. Boil for 60 minutes, adding 0.64 oz. (18 g) Fuggle and 0.64 oz. (18 g) Willamette hops, and cacao nibs at start of boil.

6. Add toasted coconut 10 minutes before flameout.

7. Add Whirlfloc tablet 10 minutes before flameout.

8. Whirlpool for 10 minutes and rest for 20 minutes.

9. Adjust post-boil volume to 5 gallons (18.9 L), if boiloff was excessive.

10. Cool wort to 68°F (20°C), then pitch White Labs WLP004 yeast at 1 million cells/ml/°P.

11. Ferment at 68°F (20°C) to completion, then rack to aging vessel.

12. Drop temperature to 39°F (4°C), add cannabis, and age until diacetyl is not detected (usually 1–2 weeks).

13. At this point, to remove the alcohol from the beer, it should be transferred back to the brew kettle and gently heated up to 173°F (78°C). If an oven is available that holds the brew kettle then that is easier to control temperature (make sure the oven's ventilation is adequate to prevent the buildup of ethanol fumes). Otherwise, a stovetop will work, but the beer should be constantly monitored to keep the beer at 173°F (78°C). The smell of alcohol coming from the brew kettle will be strong when the correct temperature is achieved. Hold the brew kettle at this temperature until the aroma of alcohol has decreased, usually within 30 minutes, then continue to hold for another 30 minutes. Remove the brew kettle from the heat and cool back to 39°F (4°C).

14. Package at 2.7 vols. CO_2.

AUTHOR COMMENTARY

This recipe gives a full-bodied milk stout with a lot of chocolate and coconut notes. The final THC content will be about 18 mg per 12-ounce bottle, which is a hefty dose and can lead to cross-fading if the alcohol is left in the beer. However, without alcohol the THC will provide a buzz similar to drinking a couple of pints of alcoholic imperial stout. This beer is a great one to sip on a cool evening before going to bed.

NA PEANUT BUTTER PORTER

Non-alcoholic dessert porter with marijuana

5 gallons (19 L)

OG: 1.055 (14°P) **IBU:** 24

FG: 1.016 (3.5°P) **ABV:** <0.5%

SRM: 48.5

MALTS AND FERMENTABLES

6.9 lb. (3.1 kg) pale malt, 2-row

0.7 lb. (0.3 kg) malted white wheat

0.9 lb. (0.4 kg) crystal 50°L

0.7 lb. (0.3 kg) crystal 75°L

0.2 lb. (0.09 kg) Baird's chocolate malt 450–550°L

HOPS

0.33 oz. (9.4 g) Chinook (12.3% AA) @ 60 min.

0.33 oz. (9.4 g) Perle (9% AA) @ 60 min.

CANNABIS

0.2 oz. (5.7 g) of decarboxylated buds at 22% THC @ dry hop

YEAST

Wyeast – 1968 London ESB Ale

ADDITIONAL ITEMS

1 lb. (454 g) peanut butter @ 15 min.

1 tablet Whirlfloc @ 10 min.

WATER

300 ppm alkalinity as $CaCO_3$

BREWING NOTES

1. Mash in malts at 1.32 qt./lb. (2.71 L/kg) at 140°F (60°C). Hold at 140°F (60°C) for 30 minutes.
2. Raise to 149°F (65°C) and hold for 10 minutes.
3. Raise to 167°F (75°C) and hold for 10 minutes for mash out conversion.
4. Sparge with 170°F (77°C) water to kettle full volume of 5.3 gallons (20 L).

5.   Boil for 60 minutes, adding 0.33 oz. (9.4 g) Chinook and 0.33 oz. (9.4 g) Perle hops at start of boil.
6.   Add peanut butter 15 minutes before kettle knockout.
7.   Add Whirlfloc tablet 10 minutes before kettle knockout.
8.   Whirlpool for 10 minutes and rest for 20 minutes.
9.   Adjust post-boil volume to 5 gallons (18.9 L), if boiloff was excessive.
10. Cool wort to 68°F (20°C) and pitch Wyeast 1968 London ESB yeast at 1 million cells/ml/°P.
11. Ferment at 68°F (20°C) to completion, then rack to aging vessel.
12. Drop temperature to 39°F (4°C), add cannabis, and age until diacetyl is not detected (usually 1–2 weeks).
13. At this point, to remove the alcohol from the beer, it should be transferred back to the brew kettle and gently heated up to 173°F (78°C). If an oven is available that holds the brew kettle then that is easier to control temperature. Otherwise, a stovetop will work, but the beer should be constantly monitored to keep the beer at 173°F (78°C). The smell of alcohol coming from the brew kettle will be strong when the correct temperature is achieved. Hold the brew kettle at this temperature until the aroma of alcohol has decreased, usually within 30 minutes, then continue to hold for another 30 minutes. Remove the brew kettle from the heat and cool back to 39°F (4°C).
14. Package at 2.7 vols. CO_2.

AUTHOR COMMENTARY

This recipe gives a full-bodied porter with roasted peanut notes. The final THC content will be about 18 mg per 12-ounce bottle, which is a hefty dose and can lead to cross-fading if the alcohol is left in the beer. However, without alcohol, the THC will provide a buzz similar to drinking a couple of pints of alcoholic imperial porter. This beer is a nice dessert beer that is reminiscent of a chocolate peanut butter cup. I tend to carbonate my porters and stouts higher than usual to help bring out the dark malt character in the aroma. As a final note, the oils in peanut butter will provide the yeast with nutrients to build cell membranes and multiply, much like the addition of oxygen. The final yeast crop will be about five times that of a normal yeast crop.

Cannabis Hard Seltzer

Hard seltzers are known as a very clean-tasting and smelling base that can be used in a number of creative beverages. For example, many companies add juices or flavors to create refreshing, low-calorie alcoholic drinks tasting like lemonade or wild berries. Others add vitamins, antioxidants, or even electrolytes to tap into the health and wellness trend that interests so many people. Still others add more alcohol, sweeteners, and flavors to mimic drinks such as hard root beer that appeal to those searching for a rewarding experience where splurging on calories does not matter.

Hard seltzer has become very popular and breweries produce many different versions to suit the desires of customers around the world. Some believe the popularity of hard seltzer is due to its gluten-free aspect or the low calorie count (generally around 100 calories per serving), while others believe the clean flavor (very little hop bitterness, if any), often highlighted with fruit and a hint of sweetness, is the driving factor. Whatever the true reason for hard seltzer's popularity, one factor is common to almost all hard seltzers on the market—a light, water-like body with no discernable malt flavor or hop bitterness. This can be traced to a loophole in TTB regulations that indicates there is no minimum usage level for malt in beverages classified as "beer" (27 C.F.R. § 25.11). Rather, the TTB allows for the use of certain other fermentable materials as a substitute for malt. One such substitute is dextrose, which results in a very clean, light flavor without the malt character found in traditional beers. The lightness of seltzers provides a base to which many flavors and ingredients can be added, including cannabinoids.

When brewing hard seltzers, other fermentables can be used to replace dextrose. Examples include candi sugar, fructose, honey, and agave syrup, to name a few. Hard seltzers made with agave are referred to as "Ranch Water" and are very popular in the state of Texas and the southwestern US. All of these alternative ingredients are highly fermentable and lend unique flavors when included in hard seltzer recipes. While powdered dextrose and fructose have minimal flavor contribution, their low moisture content makes them fairly straightforward to include in recipes because there is negligible compensation for water. Honey generally has a moisture content of 20% or less, with higher quality honeys being as low as 14% water. Recipes that include honey always have to take into consideration its moisture content to achieve accurate results in the finished product. Similar allowances should be made for agave syrup, which typically has a moisture content of 23%.

If a brewer chooses to add cannabinoids to a hard seltzer, there are several issues to consider. Brewers should consider whether the bitterness and cannabis flavor of the cannabinoids are desired or not. They should also take care to select the right preparation of cannabis to ensure any cannabinoids remain well-dispersed in the liquid throughout the beverage's shelf-life (pp. 54–58) and that any flavors they bring compliment the desired profile. In regard to bitterness, there will be additional perceived bitterness depending on the final concentration of cannabinoids in the product, which I have jokingly called cannabis bittering units, or CBUs. My own experiments have found that, despite the THC beer showing a small reduction in IBUs compared with the non-THC beer, the perception of bitterness was found to increase slightly. The possible reason for the reduction in IBUs is unknown, but it is possible that cannabinoids may "quench" any true IBU readings from isomerized alpha acids. The extra bitterness imparted by cannabinoids may or may not agree with the desired flavor profile of the product. Similar to isomerized alpha acids in beer, cannabinoids will contribute a perceived bitterness that can be minimal in low-dosed products and very assertive in heavily-dosed products. For example, my own experiments suggest an addition of 10 mg of cannabinoids will add a perceived bitterness equivalent to about 2–4 IBU, whereas the addition of 50 mg will add a perceived bitterness of about 10 IBU, along with a mild burning sensation depending on the type of emulsifier used for water solubilization. If extra bitterness is an issue, the brewer will need to incorporate compounds known as bitterness blockers to maintain the proper flavor.

Two of the oldest known substances that do the same job as bitterness blockers in foods and beverages are table sugar and salt. Sodium in salt suppresses the taste of bitterness on the tongue (Breslin and Beauchamp 1997). Interestingly, many people add salt instead of sugar to their coffee to decrease the bitterness and enhance the flavor. In the same manner, brewers can add salt to their brews to help minimize the bitterness of the final product and thereby allow other characteristics, such as hop aroma, to be maximized. Similar to salt, table sugar has also been employed to mask bitterness in food products. Sugar has been very effective over the years as a bitterness blocking agent, but sugar has slowly garnered a negative reputation as a non-healthy ingredient due to the addition of "empty" calories and the resulting spike in blood sugar levels.

Although sugar is still used in many foods and beverages to block bitterness, other promising products are being introduced to the food industry. One of these is the novel idea of mycelia from mushrooms.[7] Mycelia comprise the vegetative part of fungi. Mycelia are collected, dried, crushed into a fine powder, and mixed into a liquid form that can be added to food products during processing. This proprietary mycelia-based product binds to the bitter taste receptors on the tongue and blocks the taste of bitterness. Since the bitterness blocker only binds for about 10 seconds, it can be effective when used in beverages and foods.

Many flavor companies are working on other unique agents to block bitterness, many of which are very effective at blocking the bitterness of cannabinoids. However, the makeup of these agents is almost always proprietary or classified and they tend to be expensive or difficult for homebrewers to obtain. Professional brewers can ask their flavor suppliers for cost-effective bitterness blockers, or they can incorporate sugar if their hard seltzer product is pasteurized.

Besides the bitterness of cannabinoids, a brewer must determine if other flavors imparted by a given cannabis preparation are desirable in a hard seltzer. Much like hops, the pungent aroma of cannabis is polarizing—people either love it or hate it. Fortunately, the aromas associated with cannabis are due to the presence of terpenoids and these compounds can be selectively removed when isolating cannabinoids. A brewer can easily purchase cannabinoid distillates that are free of terpenes, where recreational marijuana is legalized.

While recipes for hard seltzers can be readily found on the internet, many factors need to be taken into consideration in order to produce satisfactory results. For instance, the use of highly fermentable sugars instead of malt can lead to sulfurous off-flavors, which must be either gassed off with generous CO_2 flushing or filtered through activated carbon. Additionally, yeast nutrients are almost always recommended to achieve consistent and complete fermentations of hard seltzer, because the absence of appropriate yeast nutrients in the fermentable substrate slows fermentative activity.

---

[7]   Chase Purdy, "Researchers have finally discovered the key to naturally stripping sugar from all our foods," Quartz, July 16, 2016, https://qz.com/732128/researchers-have-finally-discovered -the-key-to-naturally-stripping-sugar-from-all-of-our-foods/.

HARD SELTZER RECIPE
5 gallons (19 L)

OG: 1.036 (9.0°P)   **IBU:** 0
FG: 1.000 (0.0°P)   **ABV:** 4.9%
SRM: 0

MALTS AND FERMENTABLES
4.0 lb. (1.91 kg) dextrose

HOPS
(Recipe does not use hops.)

CANNABIS
0.2 oz. (5.7 g) of decarboxylated buds at 22% THC, added in fermentor

WATER
Drinking water to add to final volume of 5 gallons (19 L)

YEAST
1 packet of ale yeast specified for seltzer fermentation

ADDITIONAL ITEMS
0.06 oz. (1.6 gm) yeast nutrient [author note: adjust amount according to yeast supplier's recommendation]

BREWING NOTES
1. Add dextrose, hops (if desired), and water to brew kettle and heat with agitation to dissolve sugar solids.
2. Boil for 20 minutes to sterilize without generating excessive color.
3. Cool to 68°F (20°C) and oxygenate.
4. Pitch yeast according to supplier's recommendations. Add cannabis.
5. Ferment to completion at 68°F (20°C). Final gravity should be 1.000 (0.0°P).
6. Rack off of plant material. If required, scrub out sulfur compounds and filter for clarity.
7. Add flavorings and sweeteners as desired.

8. Carbonate to 3.0 vols. CO_2.

9. Package and pasteurize for stability. Note that preservatives such as Velcorin® can also be added in lieu of pasteurization, as long as the pH is appropriate for activation.

AUTHOR COMMENTARY

This particular seltzer recipe results in a light bodied hard seltzer containing 4.9% ABV and about 18 mg THC (assuming 20% loss) per 12-ounce serving.

10

THE ROAD
AHEAD

WHERE WE CAME FROM

As we saw in chapter 1, the history of marijuana in the United States over-laps to some extent with the history of alcohol: both products were widely consumed, then made illegal for political or monetary reasons, then made legal again when science and reason prevailed. But cannabis prohibition has lasted much longer than the 13 years it took for Prohibition to be repealed. The prohibition of cannabis under federal law has been in place since 1937, but it is quickly being eroded as more and more US states decriminalize and legalize marijuana. The waning of cannabis prohibition also mirrors that of alcohol in that it has been happening in stepwise fashion.

The end of Prohibition in 1933 occurred in two steps: at first, beer containing no more than 3.2% alcohol by weight (4% ABV) was made legal, followed by all forms of alcohol nine months later. The reason for delineating the 3.2% alcohol by weight limit was that most people thought that an alcohol content this low was not capable of making people intoxicated. It would have been interesting to interview police officers of that time period to see if any accidents involving alcohol had people who thought they could not get drunk from a few bottles of 4% ABV beer. With seemingly similar logic, in 2018 the federal government chose a maximum limit of no more than 0.3% dry weight THC when legalizing hemp under the Agriculture Improvement Act, thereby creating an arbitrary distinction between hemp and marijuana. The thinking is that anything less than 0.3% dry weight THC will not lead to intoxication, never mind that if it were made fully bioactive (i.e., THC that is fully taken up by the body such that it has a physiological effect) it would have an inebriating effect.

The need for more tax revenue was another reason for repealing Prohibition and it led to the strict regulation of alcohol sales after 1933. In a similar way, many states have legalized recreational marijuana in the hopes of increasing much needed tax revenue. Indeed, at sales tax rates approaching 30%, amid booming cannabis sales in states where it is legal, tax revenue is starting to help many financially strapped states.

WHERE WE ARE GOING

As of April 2021, marijuana was fully legalized in 16 states and the District of Columbia. It is becoming obvious from election results and national polls that the majority of people in the US think marijuana should be fully legal. To the north, Canada enjoys federal legalization of marijuana and has shown it can be regulated and made to work in the system. Meanwhile, to the south, President López Obrador and the Mexican Senate approved and passed a bill legalizing marijuana for recreational and medical use on November 19, 2020. Lawmakers in Mexico faced a December 15, 2020 deadline, issued by their supreme court, to have marijuana laws and regulations in place. However, Mexico's lower house of congress, the Chamber of Deputies, asked for an extension, which was granted by Mexico's supreme court, giving law-makers until April 30, 2021 to pass the legalization bill. The Chamber of Deputies duly passed the bill in March and returned it to the upper house. Unfortunately, the Senate then objected to amendments made to the bill and the April 30 deadline passed by without the bill being signed into law. If the bill were to pass in 2021, Mexico, with a population of almost 130 million people, would become the largest legal marijuana market in the world.

When speaking with leaders of the US and Canadian marijuana industries during 2020, many stated that they think US federal legalization will occur sometime between 2021 and 2025, with many believing it will happen by 2022.

When—not if—marijuana becomes legalized by the federal government in the US, it may resemble the structure set up in Canada. In Canada, the regulation of legal cannabis is shared by the federal, provincial, and territorial governing bodies. The federal government regulates broader legal areas such as taxation, medical cannabis, age limits, and advertising. Provincial and territorial governments regulate "local" legal issues, such as public consumption and retail regulations and locations. Most likely marijuana in the US will be highly regulated in a way very similar to alcohol, as alcohol regulations have been in place since the end of Prohibition and have worked well at generating tax revenue and ensuring quality and fairness for all industry members. "Fairness" in this context refers to large and small suppliers selling quality products to distributors and sharing in local marketing programs; distributors selling quality products from large and small suppliers to local retailers and sharing in local marketing programs; and retailers selling quality products to consumers and receiving help with setting up displays and sales programs.

The legalization and regulation of a substance (e.g., alcohol) brings benefits in terms of quality assurance and quality control, with both being paramount in the manufacturer's mind. Safety recalls can be implemented if there is a problem, and manufacturers like breweries must always ensure their product is safe to consume. Unfortunately, where regulations are not in place the results can be tragic, such as reports of mass casualties when people have purchased and consumed counterfeit alcohol that contained methanol or other poisons.[1] Injuries and fatalities from marijuana contaminated with poisons, pesticides, or other contaminants will also become a thing of the past when legalization and regulation take place. The recent spate of vaping-related deaths in the US due to vitamin E contaminants in cannabis oil serve as a deadly reminder that without full legalization and regulation, cannabis consumers are not protected to the same extent as other purchasers of consumer packaged goods.[2]

---

[1]   See, for example, Jayme Deerwester, "Costa Rica blames 19 deaths on tainted alcohol: What you need to know," *USA Today*, July 22, 2019, 10:12 a.m. ET, updated August 19, 2019, 8:58 a.m. ET, https://www.usatoday.com/story/travel/news/2019/07/22/costa-rica-blames-deaths-tainted -alcohol-methanol-what-to-know/1793061001/; and Kirk Semple, "At Least 70 Dead in Mexico From Drinking Tainted Alcohol," *New York Times*, May 13, 2020, https://www.nytimes.com/2020/05/13 /world/americas/mexico-tainted-alcohol-deaths.html.

[2]   "Outbreak of Lung Injury Associated with the Use of E-Cigarette, or Vaping, Products," Centers for Disease Control and Prevention, updated February 25, 2020, 1:00 p.m. EST, https://www.cdc.gov /tobacco/basic_information/e-cigarettes/severe-lung-disease.html.

CANNABIS RESEARCH BLOOMS

Looking beyond the legal minutiae of cannabis prohibition, the sad fact is that more than 80 years have been squandered as researchers were denied the opportunity to study the plant's potential to help humankind.

Cannabis and Medicine or Cannabis as Medicine?

The very definition of a Schedule I drug, wherein marijuana is classified, is that it has no accepted medical use and a high potential for abuse and addiction. This is belied by Epidiolex, a CBD-based drug approved by the FDA for the treatment of children with severe forms of epilepsy. Epidiolex clearly helps relieve seizure activity, much to the elation of parents who previously had no other hope for their sick children.[3]

Cancer and other diseases are areas where cannabis is being researched for potential curative actions. For example, cancerous prostate cells have increased expression of CB_1 and CB_2 receptors (*see* pp. 64–65), and stimulation of these receptors results in increased cell death and decreased prostate-specific antigen excretion, among other hopeful signs (Ramos and Bianco 2012, 3). It is possible that stimulation of these receptors with cannabinoids might result in an effective treatment. Additionally, a cannabis extract of THC and CBD was recently approved in Germany for the treatment of moderate to severe refractory spasticity in multiple sclerosis (Dariš et al. 2019, 17). Parkinson's disease is another area where cannabis has shown promise in animal studies, where it has been shown to improve bradykinesia and/or tremors (Mohanty and Lippmann 2019).

Other cannabinoids are showing promise as treatments for pain, inflammation, and other ailments. Additionally, cannabis, and more specifically cannabidiol (CBD), has shown promise in inhibiting opioid craving and possibly preventing opioid relapse (Wiese and Wilson-Poe 2018, 183). Needless to say, the future looks to be a place where cannabis might well be accepted for medical use, despite the original reasons for the DEA classifying it as a Schedule I narcotic.

As described on pages 23–24, the genes for cannabinoid biosynthesis are available to researchers. It is only a matter of time when we will see yeast that not only ferments sugars into alcohol, but also produces cannabinoids. Beer, wine, and hard seltzers will have the option of containing THC, CBD, or any mixture of cannabinoids a person desires. And, as futuristic as it sounds, cows might be cloned with the ability to produce milk with cannabinoids to help sick children. Fish, chicken,

3   Anup Patel, "A Parent's Perspective: the LGS Epidiolex Study," Epilepsy Foundation, January 27, 2018, https://www.epilepsy.com/article/2018/1/parents-perspective-lgs-epidiolex-study.

pork, and beef might also have the potential to be filled with specialty cannabinoids. Pretty much anything in the food chain that is alive and growing might have the ability to be packed with cannabinoids so that consumers can fulfill any of their health or experiential desires. The cannabis plant has and will prove useful in myriad ways.

The Future of Industry?

In addition to tax revenue, another promising area where cannabis can help society is bioplastics. As described on page 7, in 1941 the Ford Motor Company built a car body out of hemp and soy to prove that bioplastic is as durable as petroleum-based plastic. Although the December 1941 issue of *Popular Mechanics* described Ford's bioplastics car as "10 times stronger than steel" ("Pinch Hitters for Defense," p. 3), the claim was probably exaggerated to a degree. However, 78 years later, Porsche announced the launch of its newest race car made with sturdy body panels fashioned from plant fibers, including hemp.[4] As time passes, it is clear that new and renewed uses of cannabis are being applied in the modern world in successful ways. In the near future, we may see the advent of shoes, eyeglasses, bicycles, edible packaging, and many other items created using the cannabis plant.

Cannabis can be useful for industrial applications such as the production of biofuel, which is more sustainable than fossil fuel. Or, in a future when most media will be digital, the rarer print media will require paper that is of high quality and does not yellow as easily as wood pulp-based paper. Hemp is a ready source for this type of paper.

Pot in Your Pint

In the world of brewing, it is clear that cannabis can play a role in contributing flavor and effects. Although the plant has been known for centuries, it is only recently that people have discovered new ways to prepare it and use it in beverages so that it exhibits its desired properties. As emulsifying agents become more complex (pp. 56–57) it is becoming clear that THC and other cannabinoids can be delivered into the human body with precision and speed, mimicking the time it takes alcohol to enter the bloodstream after drinking. Similar emulsifiers are being researched to deliver specific hop oils into beer in ways that simulate dry hopping and result in IPAs with highly desirable aromas. It is probable that

---

[4]   "New Porsche 718 Cayman GT4 Clubsport featuring natural-fibre body panels," *Newsroom*, Porsche, March 1, 2019, https://newsroom.porsche.com/en/products/porsche-world-premiere-new-718-cayman-gt4-clubsport-16733.html.

other helpful or desirable hydrophobic compounds can be put into beers to help smooth out flavors or introduce vitamins and nutrients. Conversely, it is interesting to see that craft beer flavors are being put into marijuana edibles in at least one legal market in the US.[5]

Feed Your Mind

Beyond cannabis gummies, we may soon see craft beer flavors in cannabis ice cream, cannabis chocolates, and many other edibles made with cannabis. With new understanding of cannabinoids and the endocannabinoid system, it is also becoming clear that beers and beverages can be designed in the future to deliver specific experiences. For example, some beverages could contain cannabinoids that provide feelings of happiness and love, while others could give the user hours of alertness and energy. Others may claim to provide pain relief and sleep; still others might help with weight loss for those on a diet, or weight gain for cancer patients who have lost their appetite due to chemo.

In the end, it will be up to the public to demand better and more truthful information about the products it purchases and consumes. Since I started writing this book, there will have been millions of instances where a person consumed both alcohol and THC, but not a single instance where all the other accompanying bioactive molecules and the resulting effects were documented in any way that would further humanity's knowledge about any of this. We must figure out a way to continuously document causes and effects in such a way that we and future generations can produce trustworthy information about how products like these interact with genetics, diet, and a host of other factors.

When thinking of how to conclude this book, I was always intrigued by how Richard Brautigan finished his classic work with a word as simple yet encompassing as "mayonnaise." In the same vein, another *m* word seems like an appropriate word to end this book. Cannabis represents an enigma that has been loved, hated, prohibited, legalized, used, abused, and praised. It has made some people wealthy beyond their wildest dreams, while others serve years in prison for daring to partake. Sometime in the future, many years from now, perhaps people on this planet will wonder why there was so much fuss about marijuana.

---

[5]   Melody Baetens, "Short's Brewing teams up with dispensary for Michigan beer-flavored edibles," *Detroit News*, September 23, 2020, 3:54 p.m. ET, https://www.detroitnews.com/story /entertainment/dining/first-draft/2020/09/23/shorts-brewing-teams-up-dispensary-craft-beer -flavored-edibles/3507647001/.

GLOSSARY

bracteole
Bracteoles are small bracts that encapsulate and help protect female reproductive organs of the cannabis plant. Bracteoles in turn are surrounded and protected by bracts.

bract
Bracts are small, specialized leaves that surround the bracteole, which in turn surround the female plant's reproductive cells.

bud
The flowers of the marijuana plant that contain a high concentration of trichomes, which in turn contain most of the cannabinoids of the plant.

budtender
The person in a dispensary who waits on customers, much like a bartender in a bar. Good budtenders are usually very knowledgeable in all things cannabis.

calyx
Calyxes (or calyces) are small structures of the female cannabis flower that protect the reproductive organs, such as the pistils. Calyxes are densely covered with glandular trichomes.

cannabinoids

Chemical compounds that effect physiology by influencing CB_1 and CB_2 cell receptors in the brain and body. Endocannabinoids are produced by the body, whereas phytocannabinoids originate from the marijuana plant or other plant sources.

Cannabis

A genus in the plant family Cannabaceae. According to most current botanists, there is only one species in this genus, namely, *Cannabis sativa* L. However there are plausible arguments that other species, including *C. indica* and *C. ruderalis* likely existed in the past. However, all extant *Cannabis* plants are products of millennia of selective breeding and species-level differences almost certainly do not exist today. *C. sativa* encompasses both hemp and marijuana. Strains such as "Indica," "Sativa," and "Ruderalis" all belong to the species *Cannabis sativa* L. Interestingly, another genus in the Cannabaceae family is *Humulus*, i.e., hops.

CB_1/CB_2 receptors

Cannabinoid 1 (CB_1) receptors are believed to mediate physical and psycho-active effects in the human body, while cannabinoid 2 (CB_2) receptors are believed to mediate inflammation and immune responses.

Caryophyllene (or beta-caryophyllene)

A sesquiterpene with CB_2 receptor activity that is present and abundant in the essential oils of both hops and cannabis often in physiologically relevant concentrations. Considered a dietary cannabinoid.

CBD

Cannabidiol (CBD) is non-psychoactive and mitigates the psychoactive response of THC, among other activities. Strains of cannabis are being bred with high concentrations of CBD for consumers who wish to take advantage of the many properties of this cannabinoid.

cola

The tip of the cannabis plant's stem where flowers/buds grow together tightly. The terminal bud.

dispensary
A general term for a business that can legally sell products containing THC and other cannabinoids, whether medical or recreational.

ECS
The endocannabinoid system (ECS) is a group of receptors in the human body that make up a highly complex regulatory system that regulates physiological functions in the presence of cannabinoids. This system was discovered in the 1980s as a result of studies conducted in laboratories around the world to understand how cannabis works in the human body.

headspace analysis
A technique where a small amount of liquid, such as beer, in a sealed vial is placed inside a gas chromatography sampling device. The vial is heated, causing volatile molecules to evaporate into the headspace, and then pierced while inside the machine, and the escaping gases are captured and analyzed.

hemp
As defined by the US Food and Drug Administration, hemp is "the plant *Cannabis sativa* L. and any part of that plant, including the seeds thereof and all derivatives, extracts, cannabinoids, isomers, acids, salts, and salts of isomers, whether growing or not, with a delta-9 tetrahydrocannabinol concentration of not more than 0.3 percent on a dry weight basis."

hybrid
Hybrid refers to a cannabis plant that is a cross between two separate strains of cannabis in order to mix the preferred traits to make a highly preferred combination. It's possible that all strains in the market are hybrids.

Indica
The "Indica" strain, actually *C. sativa* var. *afghanica*, is shorter and has wider leaves than the "Sativa" strain. Traditionally, it was believed that this variety had more relaxing and sedative qualities, than "Sativa."

kief

Kief refers to the concentrated collection of trichomes from the cannabis plant and is known to contain the cannabinoids. Kief is one of the oldest known, man-made pharmaceutical preparations and is the main ingredient in hash/hashish.

live resin

Resin from freshly harvested marijuana that contains high amounts of myrcene, which has an herbal/grassy/citrus flavor.

marijuana/marihuana

As defined by the US Food and Drug Administration, "Marihuana is listed in Schedule I of the CSA due to its high potential for abuse, which is attributable in large part to the psychoactive effects of THC, and the absence of a currently accepted medical use of the plant in the United States." Often defined as cannabis that contains delta-9-tetrahydrocannabinol levels greater than 0.3% on a dry weight basis.

medical cannabis

Cannabis that is used for treating patients with debilitating medical conditions. Generally, a medical cannabis patient should be at least 18 years of age and possess a medical marijuana permit. Depending on the state, patients can legally possess up to 2 oz. (56.7 g) of flower or 1.4 oz. (40 g) of concentrate. The cost of medical cannabis is lower than recreational cannabis due to lower tax rates ranging from 0% in some states to 8.25% in Nevada. Standard servings are usually much stronger than recreational products, containing as much as 1,000 mg THC in medical edibles in Colorado.

nugs

Short for "nuggets." Another term for buds or flowers of the cannabis plant that have any leaf material trimmed and removed. The term is also used for very high quality buds.

pistil

The female sex organs of the cannabis plant. Pistils contain an ovule and two hair-like appendages called stigma. Pollen from male plants will collect on the stigma and lead to pollination.

recreational cannabis
Cannabis that is purchased in a licensed dispensary and is used by consumers aged 21 years and older where it is legal to do so. Standard servings are generally limited to no more than 10 mg THC.

Sativa
The "Sativa" strain, most likely referring to *C. sativa* var. *indica*, has tall stature and narrow leaflets, and originated in the Indian region and includes descendents in southeast Asia, Africa and the Americas. Traditionally, it was believed that this variety had more psychoactive qualities compared to "Indica."

Schedule I drug
A listing compiled by the US Drug Enforcement Agency (DEA) that contains drugs believed to have high potential for abuse and with no medical value. Examples of Schedule I drugs are ecstasy, LSD, and marijuana.

schwag
Low-quality cannabis, usually old, dry, and brown.

section 280E
Section 280E of the Internal Revenue Code makes it illegal for a business to deduct ordinary business expenses from gross income that is obtained from doing business transactions involving Schedule I and II drugs as defined in the Controlled Substances Act.

shake
The material leftover after processing buds from marijuana plants. This includes pieces of buds, but can also include leaves and some kief.

stigma
A hair-like structure that receives pollen from the male plant. Stigmas emanate from the pistils, which are located on the buds of the cannabis plant. Stigmas start out white in color and then change to brightly colored orange, yellow, red, green, or purple when the plant is mature and ready for harvest.

terpenes

The term "terpenes" is a catchall phrase for the chemical components that give cannabis and many other plants their typical aromas, such as citrus, grassy, herbal, etc. Terpenes are naturally produced by plants and are believed to attract pollinators, and they may provide protection since they are viscous, which creates a sticky surface that entraps insects (McPartland, Clarke, and Watson 2000, 22). Technically, terpenes are hydrocarbons that are classified by the number of isoprene units they contain. Terpenoids are terpenes that possess additional functional groups containing oxygen. In hops and cannabis, some of the major terpenoids are monoterpenes (containing two isoprene units) such as limonene, myrcene, and the oxygenated monoterpene linalool. Some important sesquiterpenes (containing three isoprene units) are humulene, arnesene and caryophyllene. There are hundreds of compounds identified in hops, most of which are terpenes/terpenoids (Kunze 1996, 46–47). In the US, many of the terpenes found in cannabis and other plants are considered to be Generally Recognized As Safe (GRAS) for use as food additives (Adams and Taylor 2010, 186).

THC

The psychoactive phytocannabinoid that is the most common in the marijuana plant. THC stands for delta-9-tetrahydrocannabinol.

THCA

The precursor to THC, tetrahydrocannabinolic acid must be heated to be decarboxylated into the psychoactive compound, THC.

trichomes

Glandular trichomes resemble small hairs located in the calyxes and bracts of female flowers and produce the majority of cannabinoids and terpenes. Non-glandular trichomes function to protect the plant from predators and from extreme temperatures. Trichomes start clear and slowly turn milky white or amber when the plant is ready to harvest.

trim

The leftovers from the cannabis plant when the buds have been removed. This includes stems, leaves, and some kief. This low-cost material is often extracted to obtain the THC and other cannabinoids since it is generally not smokable.

vaping

A method of consuming marijuana in which the buds or concentrate are heated to the vaporization point, and not burned, so that the vapor can be inhaled by the user.

Additional sources for information about
common cannabis-related terminology.

1. https://www.neha.org/sites/default/files/eh-topics /food-safety/Cannabis-101-Glossary-Related-Terms.pdf

2. https://www.leafly.com/news/cannabis-101 /glossary-of-cannabis-terms.

3. FDA Regulation of Cannabis and Cannabis-Derived Products, Including Cannabidiol (CBD). US Food and Drug Administration, last accessed 2/6/2021, https://www.fda.gov/news-events/public-health-focus /fda-regulation-cannabis-and-cannabis-derived-products -including-cannabidiol-cbd

BIBLIOGRAPHY

Adams, T.B., and S.V. Taylor. 2010. "Safety Evaluation of Essential Oils: A Constituent-Based Approach." In *Handbook of Essential Oils: Science, Technology, and Applications*, edited by K.H.C. Baser and G. Buchbauer, 185–208. Boca Raton, FL: CRC Press.

al-Hassan, Ahmad Y. 2001. *Technology and applied sciences*. Pt. 2, *Science and Technology in Islam*, edited by A.Y. al-Hassan, M. Ahmed, A.Z. Iskandar. Vol. 4, *The Different Aspects of Islamic Culture*. Paris: UNESCO Publishing.

Anderson, D.M., B. Hansen, D.I. Rees, J.J. Sabia. 2019. "Association of Marijuana Laws With Teen Marijuana Use: New Estimates From the Youth Risk Behavior Surveys." *JAMA Pediatrics* 173(9): 879–881. https://doi.org/10.1001/jamapediatrics.2019.1720.

Andre, Christelle M., Jean-Francois Hausman, and Gea Guerriero. 2016. "*Cannabis sativa*: The Plant of the Thousand and One Molecules." *Frontiers in Plant Science* 7:19. https://doi.org/10.3389/fpls.2016.00019.

Ben-Shabat, S., E. Fride, T. Sheskin, T. Tamiri, M.H. Rhee, Z. Vogel, T. Bisogno, L. De Petrocellis, V. Di Marzo, and R. Mechoulam. 1998. "An Entourage Effect: Inactive Endogenous Fatty Acid Glycerol Esters Enhance 2-Arachidonoyl-Glycerol Cannabinoid Activity." *European Journal of Pharmacology* 353(1): 23–31. https://doi.org/10.1016/S0014-2999(98)00392-6.

Bergamaschi, Mateus Machado, Regina Helena Costa Queiroz, Antonio Waldo Zuardi, and Jose Alexandre S. Crippa. 2011. "Safety and Side Effects of Cannabidiol, a *Cannabis sativa* Constituent." *Current Drug Safety* 6(4): 237–249. https://doi.org/10.2174/157488611798280924.

Blachly, Paul. 1976. "Effects of Decriminalization of Marijuana in Oregon." *Annals of the New York Academy of Sciences* 282: 405–415. https://doi.org/10.1111/j.1749-6632.1976.tb49913.x.

Boesen, Ulrik. 2020. *A Road Map to Recreational Marijuana Taxation*. Fiscal Fact no. 713. Tax Foundation, Washington, DC, June 9, 2020. https://taxfoundation.org/recreational-marijuana-tax/.

Bonn-Miller, Marcel O., Mallory J.E. Loflin, Brian F. Thomas, Jahan P. Marcu, Travis Hyke, and Ryan Vandrey. 2017. "Labeling Accuracy of Cannabidiol Extracts Sold Online." *JAMA* 318(17):1708–1709. https://doi.org/10.1001/jama.2017.11909.

Bouaziz, Jerome, Alexandra Bar On, Daniel S. Seidman, and David Soriano. 2017. "The Clinical Significance of Endocannabinoids in Endometriosis Pain Management." *Cannabis and Cannabinoid Research* 2(1): 72–80. http://doi.org/10.1089/can.2016.0035.

Brandeis, Jason. 2012. "The Continuing Vitality of *Ravin v. State*: Alaskans Still Have a Constitutional Right to Possess Marijuana in the Privacy of Their Homes." *Alaska Law Review* 29(2): 175–236.

Brenneisen, R. 2007. "Chemistry and analysis of phytocannabinoids and other *Cannabis* constituents." In *Marijuana and the Cannabinoids*, edited by Mahmoud A. Elsohly, 17–49. Totowa, NJ: Humana Press. https://doi.org/10.1007/978-1-59259-947-9_2.

Breslin, P., and G. Beauchamp. 1997. "Salt Enhances Flavour by Suppressing Bitterness." *Nature* 387:563. https://doi.org/10.1038/42388.

Buchbauer, G., L. Jirovetz, W. Jäger, H. Dietrich, and C. Plank. 1991. "Aromatherapy: Evidence for Sedative Effects of the Essential Oil of Lavender After Inhalation." *Zeitschrift für Naturforschung. C, Journal of Biosciences* 46(11–12): 1067–1072. https://doi.org/10.1515/znc-1991-11-1223.

Burstein, Sumner. 2015. "Cannabidiol (CBD) and Its Analogs: A Review of Their Effects on Inflammation." *Bioorganic and Medicinal Chemistry* 23(7): 1317–1385. https://doi.org/10.1016/j.bmc.2015.01.059.

Carvalho, A., E.H. Hansen, O. Kayser, S. Carlsen, F. Stehle. 2017. "Designing Microorganisms for Heterologous Biosynthesis of Cannabinoids." *FEMS Yeast Research* 17(4): fox037.

Chesney, Edward, Philip McGuire, Tom P. Freeman, John Strang, and Amir Englund. 2020. "Lack of Evidence for the Effectiveness or Safety of Over-The-Counter Cannabidiol Products." *Therapeutic Advances in Psychopharmacology* 10 (January 1): 1–13. https://doi.org/10.1177%2F2045125320954992.

Clarke, Robert C., and David P. Watson. 2007. "*Cannabis* and Natural *Cannabis* Medicines." In *Marijuana and the Cannabinoids*, edited by Mahmoud A. ElSohly, 1–16. Totowa, NJ: Humana Press.

Corsi, Daniel J., Jessy Donelle, Ewa Sucha, Steven Hawken, Helen Hsu, Darine El-Chaâr, Lise Bisnaire, Deshayne Fell, Shi Wu Wen, and Mark Walker. 2020. "Maternal Cannabis Use in Pregnancy and Child Neurodevelopmental Outcomes." *Nature Medicine* 26:1536–1540. https://doi.org/10.1038/s41591-020-1002-5.

Crombie, L., and Crombie W.M.L. 1975. "Cannabinoid Formation in *Cannabis sativa* Grafted Inter-Racially, and with Two *Humulus* Species." *Phytochemistry* 14(2): 409–412.

Currais, Anotonio, Oswald Quehenberger, Aaron M. Armando, Daniel Daugherty, Pam Maher, and David Schubert. 2016. "Amyloid Proteotoxicity Initiates an Inflammatory Response Blocked by Cannabinoids." *Aging and Mechanisms of Disease* 2:16012. https://doi.org/10.1038/npjamd.2016.12.

Dariš, Barbara, Mojca Tancer Verboten, Željko Knez, and Polonca Ferk. 2019. "Cannabinoids in Cancer Treatment: Therapeutic Potential and Legislation." *Bosnian Journal of Basic Medical Sciences* 19(1): 14–23. https://doi.org/10.17305/bjbms.2018.3532.

DEA. 2018. *The Early Years.* Drug Enforcement Administration. https://www.dea.gov/sites/default/files/2018-05/Early%20Years%20p%2012-29.pdf.

Department of Pesticide Regulation. 2017. "Legal Pest Management Practices for Cannabis Growers in California." Last modified October 9, 2017. https://www.cdpr.ca.gov/docs/county/cacltrs/penfltrs/penf2015/2015atch/attach1502.pdf.

Devane, W.A., F.A. Dysarz, M.R. Johnson, L.S. Melvin, and A.C. Howelett. 1988. "Determination and Characterization of a Cannabinoid Receptor in Rat Brain." *Molecular Pharmocology* 34(5): 605–613.

Devane, W.A., L. Hanus, A. Breuer, R.G. Pertwee, L.A. Stevenson, G. Griffin, D. Gibson, A. Mandelbaum, A. Etinger, and R. Mechoulam. 1992. "Isolation and Structure of a Brain Constituent that Binds to the Cannabinoid Receptor." *Science* 258(5090): 1946–1949. https://doi.org/10.1126/science.1470919.

ElSohly, Mahmoud A., ed. 2007. *Marijuana and the Cannabinoids.* Totowa, NJ: Humana Press.

ElSohly, Mahmoud A., Zlatko Mehmedic, Susan Foster, Chandrani Gon, Suman Chandra, and James C. Church. 2016. "Changes in Cannabis Potency Over the Last 2 Decades (1995-2014): Analysis of Current Data in the United States." *Biological Psychiatry* 79(7): 613-619. https://doi.org/10.1016/j.biopsych.2016.01.004.

Falk-Filipsson, A., A. Löf, M. Hagberg, E.W. Hjelm, and Z. Wang. 1993. "*d*-Limonene Exposure to Humans by Inhalation: Uptake, Distribution, Elimination, and Effects on the Pulmonary Function." *Journal of Toxicology and Environmental Health* 38(1): 77–88. https://doi. org/10.1080/15287399309531702.

Ferber, Sari Goldstein, Dvora Namdar, Danielle Hen-Shoval, Gilad Eger, Hinanit Koltai, Gal Shoval, Liat Shbiro, and Aron Weller. 2020. "The 'Entourage Effect': Terpenes Coupled with Cannabinoids for the Treatment of Mood Disorders and Anxiety Disorders." *Current Neuropharmacology* 18(2): 87–96. https://doi.org/10.2174/1570159X17666190903103923.

Finley, Matt. 2020. "Azulenes: A Clear Sign of Cannabis Oil Contamination." *Cannabis Science and Technology*, May 13, 2020, 52–53. https://www .cannabissciencetech.com/view/zulenes-clear-sign-cannabis-oil-contamination.

Gaoni, Y., and R. Mechoulam. 1964. "Isolation, Structure, and Partial Synthesis of an Active Constituent of Hashish." *Journal of the American Chemical Society* 86 (April 20): 1646–1647.

Gerber, Rudolph J. 2004. *Legalizing Marijuana: Drug Policy Reform and Prohibition Politics*. Westport, CT: Praeger Publishers.

Goldschmidt, Lidush, Nancy L. Day, and Gale A. Richardson. 2000. "Effects of Prenatal Marijuana Exposure on Child Behavior Problems at Age 10." *Neurotoxicology and Teratology* 22(3): 325–336. https://doi.org/10.1016 /S0892-0362(00)00066-0.

Gülck, Thies, and Birger L. Møller. 2020. "Phytocannabinoids: Origins and Biosynthesis." *Trends in Plant Science* 25(10): 985–1004. https://doi .org/10.1016/j.tplants.2020.05.005.

Guo, Yuanyuan, Jun Luo, Songwei Tan, Ben Oketch Otieno, and Zhiping Zhang. 2013. "The Applications of Vitamin E TPGS in Drug Delivery." *European Journal of Pharmaceutical Sciences* 49(2): 175–186. https://doi.org/10.1016/j.ejps.2013.02.006.

Gurgel do Vale, T., E. Couto Furtado, J.G. Santos, Jr., G.S.B. Viana. 2002. "Central Effects of Citral, Myrcene and Limonene, Constituents of Essential Oil Chemotypes from *Lippia alba* (Mill.) N.E. Brown." *Phytomedicine* 9(8): 709–714. https://doi.org/10.1078/094471102321621304.

Hartman, Rebecca L., Timothy L. Brown, Gary Milavetz, Andrew Spurgin, David A. Gorelick, Gary Gaffney, and Marilyn A. Huestis. 2015. "Controlled Cannabis Vaporizer Administration: Blood and Plasma Cannabinoids with and without Alcohol." *Clinical Chemistry* 61(6): 850–869. https://doi .org/10.1373/clinchem.2015.238287.

Hesselink, Jan M. Keppel. 2012. "New Targets in Pain, Non-Neuronal Cells, and the Role of Palmitoylethanolamide." *Open Pain Journal* 5:12–23. https://doi .org/10.2174/1876386301205010012.

Hillig, K.W. 2005. "Genetic Evidence for Speciation in *Cannabis* (Cannabaceae)." *Genetic Resources and Crop Evolution* 52: 161–180. https://doi.org/10.1007 /s10722-003-4452-y.

Horváth, Bela, Partha Mukhopadhyay, Gyorgy Haskó, and Pál Pacher. 2012. "The Endocannabinoid System and Plant-Derived Cannabinoids in Diabetes and Diabetic Complications." *American Journal of Pathology* 180(2): 432–442. https://doi.org/10.1016/j.ajpath.2011.11.003.

Hough, J.S., D.E. Briggs, R. Stevens, and T.W. Young. 1982. *Malting and Brewing Science: Volume II Hopped Wort and Beer.* 2nd ed. 1982. New York: Chapman and Hall.

Hudak, John. 2020. *Marijuana: A Short History.* Washington, DC: Brookings Institute Press.

Huestis, Marilyn A. 2007. "Human Cannabinoid Pharmacokinetics." *Chemistry and Biodiversity* 4(8): 1770–1804. https://doi.org/10.1002/cbdv.200790152.

Israel, Solomon. 2018. "The Order of Cannabis." *Winnipeg Free Press* (online), January 4, 2018. https://www.winnipegfreepress.com/arts-and-life/life /cannabis/the-order-of-cannabis-468097053.html.

Kalant, Harold. 2004. "Adverse Effects of Cannabis on Health: An Update of the Literature Since 1996." *Progress in Neuropsychopharmacology and Biological Psychiatry* 28(5): 849–863. https://doi.org/10.1016/j.pnpbp.2004.05.027.

Kohnen-Johannsen, Kathrin L., and Oliver Kayser. 2019. "Tropane Alkaloids: Chemistry, Pharmacology, Biosynthesis and Production." *Molecules* 24(4): 796. https://doi.org/10.3390/molecules24040796.

Komori, T., R. Fujiwara, M. Tanida, J. Nomura, and M.M. Yokoyama. 1995. "Effects of citrus fragrance on immune function and depressive states." *Neuroimmunomodulation* 2(3): 174–80. https://doi.org/10.1159/000096889.

Kunze, Wolfgang. 1996. *Technology Brewing and Malting*. Berlin: VLB [Versuchs- und Lehranstalt für Brauerei].

Lafaye, G., L. Karila, L. Blecha, and A. Benyamina. 2017. "Cannabis, Cannabinoids, and Health." *Dialogues in Clinical Neuroscience* 19(3): 309–316. https://doi.org/10.31887%2FDCNS.2017.19.3%2Fglafaye.

Langenheim, Jean H. 1994. "Higher Plant Terpenoids: A Phytocentric Overview of Their Ecological Roles." *Journal of Chemical Ecology* 20:1223–1280. https://doi.org/10.1007/BF02059809.

Lee, Martin A. 2012. *Smoke Signals: A Social History of Marijuana—Medical, Recreational and Scientific*. New York: Scribner.

Luo, X., M.A. Reiter, L. d'Espaux, J. Wong, C.M. Denby, A. Lechner, Y. Zhang, et al. 2019. "Complete Biosynthesis of Cannabinoids and Their Unnatural Analogues in Yeast." *Nature* 567:123–126.

Małachowska, Edyta, Piotr Przybysz, Marcin Ubowik, Marta Kucner, and Kamila Buzała. 2015. "Comparison of Papermaking Potential of Wood and Hemp Cellulose Pulps." *Annals of Warsaw University of Life Sciences – SGGW. Forestry and Wood Technology*, no. 91, 134–37.

Martin, Billy R., Raj K. Razdan, and Anu Mahadevan. 2008. Water Soluble Cannabinoids. US Patent 20080064679, filed June 23, 2005, and issued March 13, 2008.

McGovern, Patrick E. 2003. *Ancient Wine: The Search for the Origins of Viniculture*. Princeton University Press.

McElroy, W. Thomas, Jr. 2014. W. "Taxpayers Trafficking in a Schedule I or Schedule II Controlled Substance – Capitalization of Inventoriable Costs." Thomas McElroy, Jr. to Matthew A. Houtsma, December 10, 2014. Memorandum, no. 201504011. Office of Chief Counsel, Internal Revenue Service. https://www.irs.gov/pub/irs-wd/201504011.pdf.

McPartland, J.M., R.C. Clarke, and D.P. Watson. 2000. *Hemp Diseases and Pests: Management and Biological Control*. Wallingford: CABI Publishing.

McPartland J.M. 2017. "*Cannabis sativa* and *Cannabis indica* versus 'Sativa' and 'Indica'." In *Cannabis sativa L. - Botany and Biotechnology*, edited by S. Chandra, H. Lata, M. ElSohly, 101–121. Cham, Switzerland: Springer. https://doi.org/10.1007/978-3-319-54564-6_4.

McPartland, J.M. 2018. "*Cannabis* Systematics at the Levels of Family, Genus, and Species." *Cannabis and Cannabinoid Research* 3(1): 203–212. https://doi.org/10.1089/can.2018.0039.

Mechoulam, R., and Y. Shvo. 1963. "Hashish—I. The Structure of Cannabidiol." *Tetrahedron* 19(12): 2073–2078.

Mohanty, Diksha, and Steven Lippmann. 2019. "Marijuana for Parkinson's Disease?" *Innovations in Clinical Neuroscience* 16(1–2): 33–34.

Nasaw, David. 2000. *The Chief: The Life of William Randolph Hearst*. Boston : Houghton Mifflin.

Neve, R.A. 1991. *Hops*. London: Chapman and Hall.

Nuutinen, Tarmo. 2018. "Medicinal Properties of Terpenes Found in *Cannabis sativa* and *Humulus lupulus*." *European Journal of Medicinal Chemistry* 5:198–228. https://doi.org/10.1016/j.ejmech.2018.07.076.

Pacher, Pál, Sándor Bátkai, and George Kunos. 2006. "The Endocannabinoid System as an Emerging Target of Pharmacotherapy." *Pharmacological Reviews* 58(3): 389–462. https://doi.org/10.1124/pr.58.3.2.

Pazouki, Leila, and Ülo Niinemets. 2016. "Multi-Substrate Terpene Synthases: Their Occurrence and Physiological Significance." *Frontiers in Plant Science* 7:1019. https://doi.org/10.3389/fpls.2016.01019.

Peng, Yuan Wei, Ediriweera Desapriyab, Herbert Chan, and Jeffrey R. Brubacher. 2020. "Residual Blood THC Levels in Frequent Cannabis Users after over Four Hours of Abstinence: A Systematic Review." *Drug and Alcohol Dependence* 216 (November 1): 108177. https://doi.org/10.1016/j.drugalcdep.2020.108177.

Pertwee, Roger G. 1997. "Pharmacology of Cannabinoid CB_1 and CB_2 Receptors." *Pharmacology and Therapeutics* 74(2):129-80. https://doi.org/10.1016/s0163-7258(97)82001-3.

Popescu, Viorica, Alina Soceanu, Simona Dobrinas, and Gabriela Stanciu. 2013. "A Study of Beer Bitterness Loss During the Various Stages of the Romanian Beer Production Process." *Journal of the Institute of Brewing* 119(3): 111–115. https://doi.org/10.1002/jib.82.

Ramos Juan A., and Fernando J. Bianco. 2012. "The Role of Cannabinoids in Prostate Cancer: Basic Science Perspective and Potential Clinical Applications." *Indian Journal of Urology* 28(1): 9–14. https://doi.org/10.4103/0970-1591.94942.

Rosenthal, Ed, and Unknown Brewer. 1996. *Marijuana Beer: How to Make Your Own Hi-Brew Beer.* 2nd ed. Oakland: Quick American Archives.

Russo, Ethan B. 2011. "Taming THC: Potential Cannabis Synergy and Phytocannabinoid-Terpenoid Entourage Effects." *British Journal of Pharmacology* 163(7):1344-1364. https://doi.org/10.1111/j.1476-5381.2011.01238.x.

Salles, Évila Lopes, Hesam Khodadadi, Abbas Jarrahi, Meenakshi Ahluwalia, Valdemar Antonio Paffaro Jr., Vincenzo Costigliola, Jack C. Yu, David C. Hess, Krishnan M. Dhandapani, and Babak Baban. 2020. "Cannabidiol (CBD) Modulation of Apelin in Acute Respiratory Distress Syndrome." *Journal of Cellular and Molecular Medicine* 24(21): 12869–12872. https://doi.org/10.1111/jcmm.15883.

Seltenrich, N. 2019. "Cannabis Contaminants: Regulating Solvents, Microbes, and Metals in Legal Weed." *Environmental Health Perspectives* 127(8): 082001. https://doi.org/10.1289%2FEHP5785.

Sharkey, Keith A., Nissar A. Darmani,, and Linda A. Parker. 2014. "Regulation of Nausea and Vomiting by Cannabinoids and the Endocannabinoid System." *European Journal of Pharmacology* 722 (January 5): 134–146. https://doi.org/10.1016/j.ejphar.2013.09.068.

Small, Ernest, and Arthur Cronquist. 1976. "A Practical and Natural Taxonomy for Cannabis." *Taxon* 25, no. 4 (August): 405–435.

Vallianou, Ioanna, Nikolaos Peroulis, Panayotis Pantazis, and Margarita Hadzopoulou-Cladaras. 2011. "Camphene, a Plant-Derived Monoterpene, Reduces Plasma Cholesterol and Triglycerides in Hyperlipidemic Rats Independently of HMG-CoA Reductase Activity." *PLoS ONE* 6(11): e20516. https://doi.org/10.1371/journal.pone.0020516.

Villa, Keith, and Catherine Villa. 2020. "Prevention and Reversal of the Formation of Light-Struck (3-Methyl-2-Butene-1-Thiol) Aroma in Beer." e-Poster presented at the World Brewing Congress WBC Connect 2020 [online meeting], September 19, 2020. https://brewing.confex.com/brewing/2020/meetingapp.cgi/Paper/1466.

Vitale, Stephen A., and Jospeh L. Katz. 2003. "Liquid Droplet Dispersions Formed by Homogeneous Liquid–Liquid Nucleation: 'The Ouzo Effect.'" *Langmuir* 19(10): 4105–4110. https://doi.org/10.1021/la026842o.

Volkow, Nora D, Ruben D. Baler, Wilson M. Compton, and Susan R.B. Weiss. 2014. "Adverse Health Effects of Marijuana Use." *New England Journal of Medicine* 370(23): 2219–2227. https://doi.org/10.1056/NEJMra1402309.

Wang, Mei, Yan-Hong Wang, Bharathi Avula, Mohamed M. Radwan, Amira S. Wanas, John van Antwerp, Jon F. Parcher, Mahmoud A. ElSohly, and Ikhlas A. Khan. 2016. "Decarboxylation Study of Acidic Cannabinoids: A Novel Approach Using Ultra-High-Performance Supercritical Fluid Chromatography/Photodiode Array-Mass Spectrometry." *Cannabis and Cannabinoid Research* 1(1): 262–271. https://doi.org/10.1089/can.2016.0020.

Westin, A.A., G. Mjønes, O. Burchardt, O.M. Fuskevåg, and L. Slørdal. "Can Physical Exercise or Food Deprivation Cause Release of Fat-Stored Cannabinoids?" *Basic and Clinical Pharmacology Toxicology* 115(5): 467–471. https://doi.org/10.1111/bcpt.12235.

WHO. 2017. *Cannabidiol (CBD): Pre-Review Report.* Agenda Item 5.2, Expert Committee on Drug Dependence, 39th Meeting, Geneva, November 6–10, 2017. World Health Organization. https://www.who.int/medicines/access /controlled-substances/5.2_CBD.pdf.

Wiese, Beth, and Adrianne R. Wilson-Poe. 2018. "Emerging Evidence for Cannabis' Role in Opioid Use Disorder." *Cannabis and Cannabinoid Research* 3(1): 179–189. https://doi.org/10.1089/can.2018.0022.

Yang, M-Q., R. van Velzen, F.T. Bakker, A. Sattarian, D-Z. Li, T-S Yi. 2013. "Molecular Phylogenetics and Character Evolution of Cannabaceae." *Taxon* 62(3): 473–485. https://doi.org/10.12705/623.9.

INDEX

United States Patent and Trademark
  Office (USPTO), 53, 95
US Constitution, 82
US Department of Agriculture, 110
US Department of the Treasury, 5, 17
US Drug Enforcement Administra-
  tion (DEA), 8, 10, 75, 76
US Food and Drug Administration
  (FDA), 18, 57, 162; CBD and, 59,
  77, 78, 95–96; health claims and,
  60; jurisdiction of, 75–76
US Supreme Court, 10
USDA, 76
USPTO. *See* United States Patent and
  Trademark Office

vaping, defined, 173
vegetable gum, 55
vegetative stage, 35; described,
  36–37; photo of, 36
Vertosa, 61
vitamins, 56, 153, 161, 164

Wang, Mei, 113
warning labels, 92–93; THC, 92, 93,
  93 (fig.)
Washington, George, 121
water, 1–9; compatibility, 56–58; ion-
  ized, 108
weizenbock, 139–40
white supremacy, 7
World Health Organization, 65
wort, 105, 106, 124, 126
Wyden, Ron, 13

xanthan gum, 54
XO lids, 96, 97; photo of, 97

yeast, 108, 109, 119, 120; nutrients,
  155; specialty, 105, 106–7

Zygosaccharomyces rouxii, 106